The
TANTRIC DAKINI
ORACLE

Also by Nik Douglas and Penny Slinger

The Erotic Sentiment: In the Paintings of China and Japan

The Erotic Sentiment: In the Paintings of India and Nepal

Sexual Secrets Twentieth Anniversary Edition:
The Alchemy of Ecstasy

The Path of the Mystic Lover: Baul Songs of Passion and Ecstasy
(with Bhaskar Bhattacharyya)

The TANTRIC DAKINI ORACLE

ORACLE

Nik Douglas
and
Penny Slinger

Destiny Books
Rochester, Vermont

Destiny Books
One Park Street
Rochester, Vermont 05767
www.InnerTraditions.com

Destiny Books is a division of Inner Traditions International

Originally published in 1979 by Destiny Books under the title *The Secret Dakini Oracle*. Cards originally published in 1982 by U.S. Games Systems, Inc., under the title *The Secret Dakini Oracle Deck*.

Library of Congress Cataloging-in-Publication Data
Douglas, Nik.
    The Tantric Dakini oracle / Nik Douglas and Penny Slinger.
        p. cm.
    ISBN 978-0-89281-137-3
    1. Tarot. 2. Tarot cards. 3. Tantrism. I. Slinger, Penny. II.
Title.
    BF1879.T2D695 2003
    133.3'2424—dc21

                                        2003013166

Printed and bound in China

10 9 8 7 6 5 4

Text design and layout by Priscilla Baker and Mary Anne Hurhula
This book was typeset in Galliard with Albertus, Isadora, and Jante as the display typefaces.

*"Look into the mirror of your mind,
The home of the Secret Dakini."*

The Great Secret Dakini. This is a form of the Dakini Vajravarahi, a mystic aspect
of gnosis, here depicted in the traditional form. The sculpture is of wood,
in relief, and is from Tibet, circa eighteenth century.

Contents

$\mathcal{P}$reface

The Tantric Dakini Oracle is an ancient concept of psychic divination brought into contemporary form. The cards which make up the Oracle can be used in a number of different ways, both for divination and as an aid in personality transformation. *The Tantric Dakini Oracle* works on many different levels and the powerful symbolism of the cards can enhance the psychic faculties of clairvoyance and visualization.

All mystical and alchemical treatises are concerned with transformation. For years the idea of an individual's conscious transformation appealed to me as the surest way to achieve goals which are beyond the range of any fixed personality. I journeyed to the East and spent many years there exploring the mystery-teachings and especially the Tantras. The texts known as the Tantras, more than any other teachings, affirm that conscious transformation is an evolutionary act.

My studies of yoga and tantra introduced me to the concept of the dakini. A dakini is an archetype of feminine wisdom-energy. Traditionally there are sixty-four dakinis which are believed to be expressions of archetypal energies within every human being. Dakinis are said to be sometimes creative and sometimes destructive, and without their different energies we would cease to exist. The dakini concept is paramount in the yoga and tantra mysteries.

I traced references to dakini temples and managed to locate the most ancient of them, Ranipur Jharial, in the Sambalpur region of Orissa, India. This temple was built in the eighth century, at the height of the tantric period, and was used as a place of initiation. By the fifteenth century it had become disused and forgotten but was rediscovered in 1879.

With great difficulty I managed to reach this temple of the sixty-four dakinis. The building was positioned on the top of a huge black rock rising upward from the shores of a small lake. The temple is made of sandstone, with tapered walls and a single entrance leading into a circular enclosure open to the sky. At the center was a single dancing male figure, Shiva, and in separate niches or cloisters around the inner circumference were sixty-four dancing female figures, the shaktis, or dakinis.

The temple of Ranipur Jharial illustrates perfectly the concept of psychic transformation as described in the Tantras. It outlines the basic metaphysics of the transformation teachings: sixty-four energies, personalized as dancing goddesses, either peaceful or wrathful, bearing weapons, symbols and making gestures. Like passengers within a great flying saucer, these figures surround the central axis, Shiva. The temple became better known to me after I had made detailed measurements and studied the iconographies of the figures and compared my findings with esoteric teachings found in the yoga and tantra mystic traditions. That a temple of the eighth century could so precisely illustrate the concepts of psychic transformation found in the tantric texts became a source of inspiration as well as an obsession. I searched out, located and studied four other dakini temples and made detailed comparisons.

In my studies I discovered that the dakini temple of Ranipur Jharial was considered the original teaching-place of the Tantras, a teaching in stone illustrating both the cycles of transformation and the paths of destiny. Early texts refer to "the magical land of Shambala, to the Northwest of the Kingdom of Uddiyana"; other texts refer to the king of Shambala as Indrabhuti. I was able to locate King Indrabhuti in Orissa, to the northwest of which I found mod-

ern Sambalpur with the circular Ranipur Jharial temple of the dakinis. The *Kalachakra Tantra*, a major text dealing with the cycles of
transformation, was said to have been developed in Shambala itself
by the great tantric master, Pitopa. It is the *Kalachakra Tantra*
which relates the inner energy centers (chakras) of the subtle, or
yoga, body to the outer spheres, the natural rhythms and cycles
found in the external world of phenomena. The sixty-four dakini
temple is a direct expression of this concept, and *The Tantric Dakini
Oracle* is a contemporary form of these ancient wisdom-teachings.

The Dakinis in the Tantric Tradition

One of the most interesting references to the dakini concept is to
be found in the life story of Guru Padmasambhava, who first
brought the tantric teachings to Tibet in the eighth century (the
period of the Ranipur Jharial temple in Sambalpur district). The
standard text relates how Padmasambhava spent some time "in the
land of Shambala, where he learned the *Kalachakra Tantra* and
other mystic transmissions." The story tells how he received his
final initiation.

> Padma's initiation was through an-ordained Dakini who
> dwelt in a sandalwood garden in the midst of a cemetery, in
> a palace of skulls. When he arrived at the door of the palace
> he found it closed, but then there appeared a servant woman
> carrying water. Padma sat in meditation so that her water-
> carrying was halted by his Yogic power. Thereupon, taking a
> knife of crystal, she cut open her breast and exhibited within
> it the peaceful and wrathful deities, dancing in a circle.
> Addressing Padma she said, "I observe that you are a good
> Yogi. But look, have you not faith in me?" Padma bowed
> down and requested her teachings. She replied, "I am only
> a maid-servant. Come inside."

> Upon entering the palace Padma saw the great Secret Dakini
> sitting on a sun and moon throne, holding in her hands a
> double drum and a bowl made of a skull, and surrounded by
> Dakinis, all of which were making Tantric offerings and ges-
> tures to her. Padma made proper obeisance to the
> enthroned Dakini and begged her to teach him both esoter-
> ically and exoterically. The peaceful and wrathful deities then
> appeared in a circle overhead. "Behold," said the Dakini,
> "these are the deities; now take initiation."

The Tantras affirm that the divine is to be found within each
personalized aspect of the individual self and that the visionary
process is the most direct way of experiencing the divinity within. By
visualization and introspection the self can be taken out of time-limitations and moved into a place of existence in the eternal present.
There are numerous and varied tantric teachings centered around
concepts of a particularized evocation brought into effect by visual-
izing power symbols. Such visualization acts as a potent means of
channeling and transforming archetypal energies from deep within
the psyche. The dakinis are particularized distillations of archetypal
energies. For example, in an esoteric text known as the *Yoga of the
Psychic Heat* there is the following illuminating description of the
Red Dakini, Vajravarahi:

> Imagine thyself to be the Divine devotee, the Vajra Dakini,
> red of color; as effulgent as the radiance of a ruby; having
> one face, two hands and three eyes. The right hand holds
> aloft a brilliantly gleaming curved knife, flourishing it high
> overhead, cutting off completely all mentally disturbing
> thought processes. The left hand holds against her breast a
> skull-bowl filled with nectar, giving satisfaction with her
> inexhaustible Bliss. She has a tiara of skulls on her head, she

wears fifty human heads as a garland and has five of the six traditional symbolic ornaments, the cemetery-dust being missing. In the bend of her left arm she holds a long mystic staff, symbolizing the Divine Father-essence, the Heruka. She is nude, in the full bloom of virginity, at the sixteenth year of her age, dancing with the right leg bent and the foot uplifted, the left foot treading upon the breast of a prostrate human form. Visualize her as being thyself, externally in the shape of a deity and internally as altogether vacuous like the inside of an empty sheath, transparent and uncloudedly radiant; vacuous even to the fingertips, like an empty tent of red silk, or like a filmy tube distended with breath. At the start let the visualization be about the size of your own body; then as big as a house; then as large as a hill; and finally, vast enough to contain the Universe. Then concentrate the mind upon it. Next reduce it gradually, little by little, to the size of a sesame seed, then to the size of a very greatly reduced sesame seed, still having all the limbs and parts of the Dakini sharply defined. Upon this too, concentrate the mind.

SECRET TEACHINGS OF NAROPA

The Dakinis in *The Tantric Dakini Oracle*

The archetypal forms of the dakinis have been interpreted in a contemporary context. By making use of collage techniques, Penny Slinger and myself have blended together symbols and archetypes into a new presentation of the Kalachakra (Wheel of Time) wisdom-cycle which works on both conscious and unconscious levels of perception. The cards are a mirroring device, effectively evoking subtle memories, sentiments, desires or fears. By knowing what the influences are which are related to any particular moment of time it is possible then to transform destiny. *The Tantric Dakini Oracle* deck is a cycle of sixty-four archetypes conceived of as moving around a central point, the self. Such a concept is found throughout all ancient occult traditions, but nowhere is it more clearly expressed than in the Tantras.

The Tantric Dakini Oracle and the Tarot

There is a direct relationship between *The Tantric Dakini Oracle* cards and the Tarot. Though we did not set out to create a "Tantric Tarot" the final result has been a total and natural synthesis of the tantric teachings and the Tarot. Twenty-two of the cards directly relate to the Major Arcana cards of the traditional Tarot. The next forty cards symbolize the four elements—Air, Fire, Water and Earth, with ten cards to each element; this is similar to the four suits of the Minor Arcana of the Tarot. Finally there are three "time" cards, representing the Past, Present and Future.

The origins of the Tarot are lost in antiquity. The earliest cards which have survived are almost definitely from the fourteenth century and have a consistently Eastern emphasis in design and symbolism. Esoteric Western traditions tell of the Tarot cards evolving from ancient Egypt or of their being brought to Europe by the Gypsies, who came from India. Our purpose here is not to enter into lengthy discussions about the possible origins of the Tarot cards or the reason why so much of their symbolism can be understood from an understanding of tantra. We know that in India there is strong evidence suggesting early contact with the priesthoods of Egypt: an exchange of esoteric ideas must certainly have taken place.

The Tantric Dakini Oracle has a practical application for each person and offers a means to better understand and control one's own destiny.

NIK DOUGLAS

A dakini from the Hirapur circular temple. Lion-headed, this archetype relates to card #62, Dangerous Pussy, and both protects the cycle of dakinis and represents the power of the past. Orissa, India, circa 900.

PART I

Consulting the Oracle

A dakini from the Tibetan tradition. This form has evolved out of the Hirapur cycle of dakinis. It is the Tibetan form of Senge Dolma, the Protector of the Past. Circa seventeenth century.

$\mathcal{I}$ntroduction to the Oracle

The ancient occult teachings of the great tantric masters of the East contain knowledge of the inner mysteries of the universe. The sixty-five cards comprising *The Tantric Dakini Oracle* are surrealistic expressions of each of these inner mysteries found in the subtle body, or yoga body.

Man and woman are like mirrors of the universe, or macrocosm the world outside. Inner and outer are in truth not separate, but interwoven, forming a fabric of existence which extends from the spiritual to the material. If we search within ourselves, we find that we are composed of the same basic principles and substances that are found in the realities of the outside world. The atom and its orbital particles, all cells, tissues, molecules, the elements, the sun, the planets and the galaxies are like multiple reflections of one greater unity which pervades everything. We can experience this unity by coming to know our inner self, and this can be achieved through familiarity with the component parts of the self.

According to Eastern tradition, the Secret Dakinis guard the deeper mysteries of the self. These Secret Dakinis, generally believed to be sixty-four in number, are understood to be symbolic representations of gnosis, the female principle of transforming wisdom, and to act on the Navel or Solar Plexus of the physical body. As personifications of the feminine wisdom-essence, the Secret Dakinis bring about a transformation at this center. Thus they can be likened to the

WISH-GRANTING GEM. These sixty-four wisdom energies, as archetypes of vitality, take on the dance of life around the self, bringing about an evolutionary transformation which extends into the spiritual realms. The psychic center at the Navel plays a significant role in all esoteric practices which have self-transformation as their goal. The dakinis represent the ever-changing play of forces at the Navel center. Understanding this concept is of paramount importance in the development and ultimate evolution of the human psyche.

All psychological components of personality exist as energies at the Navel center and can be transformed by a process of evocation and introspection. *The Tantric Dakini Oracle* cards can assist personality transformation by acting as mirrors in this process. The sixty-four primordial energies can be better understood by knowing their symbolic representations.

The Secret Dakinis are traditionally likened to the flames of an inner sun, located at the Navel center. As every student of the occult will discover, this inner fire of extracted vitality principles, concentrated around the Navel center, may be used to burn up negative attitudes that perpetuate karma and destiny, thus clearing the way for spiritual fulfillment. According to the tantric tradition, the fire at the Navel center, can be put to use in the service of conscious evolution. Properly directed through meditation and visualization, it can burn up the ego, with all its attendant personality problems. The Head or lunar center comes into play in this transmutative process by distilling into cooling, lunar water (symbolic of spirituality) the remnant of ego and negativity which the solar fire has burnt up. This inner process of personality distillation brings about a total transformation of the psyche. Solar-lunar symbolism permeates all occult doctrines, but the Eastern tantric teachings, in particular, have fully extended and developed the concept, elaborating the micro-macrocosmic relationship and the flow of solar and lunar energies within the subtle body.

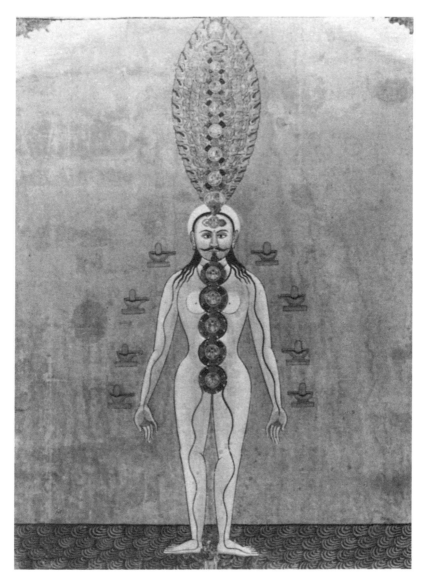

The yoga body of the tantric tradition. Showing stages of evolution and the psychic centers (chakras). Painting from Nepal, courtesy David Tremayne Ltd. Circa 1780.

The Tantric Dakini Oracle reveals, through a deck of sixty-five transcendental visionary cards, the surface of reality at the moment of consultation. Whatever question is brought to mind at this moment may be read through the order and placement of the cards, which provide a clear picture of the dominant influences and potential outcomes of the consultation.

The flow and concentrations of influencing energies are indicated by the archetypal images evoked by the cards themselves, opening the doorways through to the three "times," namely past, present and future. *The Tantric Dakini Oracle* deck is a study of transformation. Each individual card represents, in a surrealistic mode, a particular aspect of transcendent reality. The cards are expressions of the collective gnosis and each card symbolically represents an aspect of the dakinis, the energies of the transformation center. Practice with the cards and concentration on their imagery will assist the intuition in perceiving the subconscious influences underlying destiny.

An ancient tantric aphorism declares:

> Look into the mirror of your mind,
> The home of the Secret Dakini.

The Tantric Dakini Oracle explores this potent truth, providing a method of "mirroring" into the mind in order to discover the secrets of the dakinis, the energies of transformation.

The two charts, the Tree of Life and the Great Universe Map, present powerful visual pictures of mystical reality. These tantric charts are separate and independent systems for consulting the Oracle, but, for the fullest possible reading, they may be used sequentially. The Tree of Life depicts the subtle body of the yoga philosophy with psychic centers, or chakras, designated according to authentic Eastern tradition. The chart is in effect a synthesis of the Semitic Tarot divination and the Eastern tantric teachings on the subtle body. The second chart, Great Universe Map, shows the cards in an astrological configuration and may be used to determine

future events according to standard astrological methods of interpretation. Here again we have a synthesis of East and West, for the
chart is presented in the traditional Eastern way, with particular
emphasis on the intimacy of the individual mystic universe. Both
charts are truly extraordinary and authentic tantric art objects, visu-
ally powerful and of profound esoteric content. The elements, energies, currents, concentrations and fulfillments of authentic existence
are indicated by the relationships of the cards to each other and their
placement on the charts—the Tree of Life or Great Universe Map.
The synchronistic relationship between the pattern in which the
cards fall and the pattern of forces in our destiny at the same moment
allows us to explore our destiny through the use of the cards as an
oracle, similar to the original Tarot of the Egyptians, the Kabbala of
the Hebrews and the I Ching of the Chinese. An interesting parallel can be made with the I Ching, or Book of Changes, which uses
a system based on a cyclical concept of sixty-four changing energies.
This system is also centered on the philosophical conception of
personal transformation through the Navel center. Recent compar-
ative research in this area suggests that there was in fact a consider-
able exchange of ideas between Chinese and Indian occult systems
during the early period of their systemization.

The Tantric Dakini Oracle is a contemporary expression of the
innermost tantric teachings concerned with transformation.
Correctly used, it points out the relationships between past, present
and future, the cycles of time and destiny, the recurring factors
which make up what is known as fate, and the means of transcending dualistic limitations. The cards work primarily on the intuitive
level. All occult teachings stress the necessity for the integration of
polarities in spiritual development. The Chinese express the basic
polarity in the concepts of yang and yin, the archetypal male and
female principles. In the tantric traditions of India and Tibet, these
same principles are recognized as underlying all phenomena and are

named shiva and shakti. On the chart of the Tree of Life, these two principles are symbolized by the images depicted on the right and left sides of the Tree, such as day and night, flowers and beasts, and so forth. *The Tantric Dakini Oracle* authentically represents the inherent unity of all dualities and draws inspiration directly from the archetypes within each of us.

Approaching the Oracle

In any consultation, the first requirement is for the questioner to develop a rapport with the cards. This rapport is necessary to manifest the inherent synchronism between the questioner and cards as they are laid out for the reading. Therefore, treat the reading as a personal ceremony. Ideally, the questioner will clear his mind by means of a short period of meditation and then focus his concentration on the particular question which he wishes to ask of the oracle. Either the questioner can shuffle and lay out the cards for himself or, alternately, a reader may handle the interpretation and divination. However, if the questioner is present, he must be the one to shuffle and cut the cards. If the cards are being read for an absent person, then the shuffling is best done by a close acquaintance, who should concentrate on and repeat the name of the person while shuffling and cutting the deck.

The full deck of sixty-five cards is placed in numerical order from 0 to 64, so as to start from a constant point of reference. The questioner shuffles the deck maintaining direct contact with the cards. Machine shuffling devices should be avoided when consulting *The Tantric Dakini Oracle*. A particularly suitable method of laying out the cards is to place them on the floor or table, moving them around with circular sweeps. Take care to maintain the maximum amount of contact with the cards and at the same time achieve a good shuffle. When the questioner feels that the cards have been adequately shuffled, he stacks them together in a pile. Once again, since the purpose of this handling is to invest the cards with as much personal vibration as possible, it is important to maintain a suitable mental attitude and concentration on the question.

Using the *left hand only*, the questioner cuts the deck into three piles and puts the piles back together again at random. This procedure is then repeated two more times, making nine cuts of the shuffled deck in total. The complete deck is then handed to the reader, if there is one; if the questioner is reading for himself, he proceeds on his own. Actually, the best results are obtained if a second party does the reading.

The top ten cards are turned over, one at a time, and can be laid out in a variety of ways. For those readers already familiar with the Tarot, laying them out in a Celtic Cross will prove the simplest method and enable the reader to make connections between the two systems, wherever relevant. Then the same cards may be transferred to the Tree of Life chart to obtain a total picture of the Oracle's answer with respect to the subtle body. Alternately, for those who are unfamiliar with the Tarot method, it will be advantageous to lay the cards directly onto the Tree of Life chart. In both cases, the reader, while laying out the cards, should state aloud the meaning of the location of each card and its relation to the card's symbolism.

The layout of the cards on the chart presents a visual diagram of the Oracle's answer and an image of the psychological attitude of the person consulting it. The reading and interpretation of the cards can then proceed on many levels, from the intuitive to the more complex analytical and symbolic meanings. It will be found that certain cards evoke particular reactions in the participant (this reaction varies from person to person), leading to an awareness of the meaning behind the images.

The layout of the cards on the Tree of Life chart is a diagnosis of the dominant influences, concentrations and potentialities present during the magical act of consulting *The Tantric Dakini Oracle*.

The subtle centers of the yoga body, the chakras of Eastern occultism, are indicated on the chart as card places. The location of specific cards at any given center shows the state of the psychic energies at that center and indicates whether the energy potential is moving in an upward or downward direction. The section dealing with the individual cards details the meaning of the symbolism and the different readings possible according to the varied locations on the chart. The numerological connotations and the interaction of *The Tantric Dakini Oracle* with the traditional Tarot are also supplied. All these factors enter into a complete reading. Reading the Tree of Life chart should be approached from the intuitive level of awareness.

A third method of laying out the cards employs the other chart, the Great Universe Map. Here the cards are shuffled, cut and then laid directly onto the chart, in a counter-clockwise direction, starting at the point marked Aries and continuing around through to Pisces. The thirteenth card, representing the self, is placed at the central position. The map then presents a picture of the opposing and complementary forces acting on the questioner, from the point of view of astrology. Interpretations should be made according to the standard methods of astrology.

Contemplation on and use of the cards can actually stimulate a conscious awakening of these same psychic centers and lead to a deeper degree of meditation. The cards have real magical potency in their visual blending of the archetypes they represent. The brief lines of text on the cards encapsulate the essence of the transformation that each card evokes.

Method of the Celtic Cross

As previously stated, the cards are placed in sequence, thoroughly shuffled, cut into three and then stacked together again. The cutting of the deck into three piles and restacking is repeated two more times. The deck, placed face down on the table or floor is now ready for spreading and interpretation. See Figure 1 for the initial layout. The reader turns over the top card and states aloud:

This card covers you and represents the situation surrounding you. The next card is then turned over and laid across the first, with the words:

This card crosses your previous card and represents the opposing forces of good or evil, the "positivity" or "negativity" influencing you.

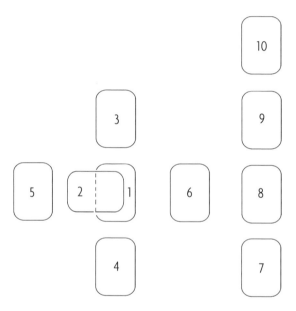

Figure 1. Initial Celtic Cross Layout

The third card is turned over and placed directly above the first card, with the words:

This represents your conscious thoughts on the matter.
The fourth card is next turned over and placed below the first card with the words:

This card represents your unconscious thoughts on the matter.

The fifth card is turned over and placed to the left side of the original card, with the words:

This card represents the influences that have just passed out of your life or which are in the process of passing.

The sixth card is placed to the right of the first card, so that the whole layout takes the form of a cross, with the first card at the center. Say the words:

This card represents the influences coming into your life, the future.

Next, the seventh card is turned over and placed on the location indicated in the diagram, with the words:

This represents your self.

The eighth card is turned over and placed next to the seventh card, as in the diagram, with the words:

This card represents the environment which you inhabit.

The ninth card is turned over, with the words:

This card represents your hopes and expectations.

Finally, the tenth card is turned over and placed alongside the ninth, eighth and seventh cards, forming a single line, with the words:

This card represents the final outcome, and is the answer to your question.

Method of the Tree of Life Chart

In order to transpose a simple Tarot type of reading to the Tree of Life chart of the subtle body, the cards are turned, as indicated in the second diagram, Figure 2, and moved to their correct locations on the Tree of Life, as in Figure 3 (to order the Tree of Life chart, see page 207).

Those who are not familiar with the Tarot may place the cards directly on the correct locations on the chart, once the shuffling and cutting has been completed. The advantage of this direct method is that practicing it will enable you to grasp the concept of the Tree of Life, quickly strengthening your understanding of the symbolic meanings behind the cards and the chart.

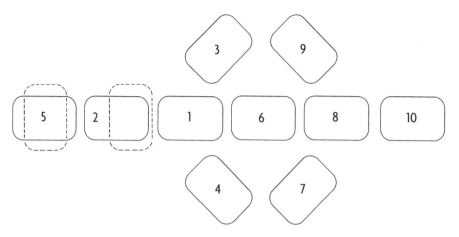

Figure 2. The cards turned ready to be moved to placement on Tree of Life Chart

What follows is a brief interpretation of the meaning behind the card locations or psychic centers of the subtle body. This subject is further treated in the interpretations of the individual cards. The reading of *The Tantric Dakini Oracle* cards through their location on the chart of the Tree of Life shows in tantric terms the situation with regard to the subtle centers (chakras), their functions and influences.

Base Center. The fifth of the cards is placed at the Base center, which is related to the Earth element, around which the roots of the Tree of Life are entwined. Within this center, which is reddish in color, is depicted a standing elephant headed figure, who is the Hindu god Ganesha, the Lord of All Obstacles and ruler of the Base region. He stands on the figures of Radha and Krishna, the Divine Lovers, who are shown in passionate embrace, symbolizing that love is the force which drives the psyche upward. Their passion stimulates the inner psychic fire, the inner heat, symbolized by the serpents. The serpent energy, called kundalini, is the energy of transformation, which rises upward in the Tree of Life, piercing the other centers. This card place indicates the raw energies, the passed or passing influences, related to the world and all earthly things. It is

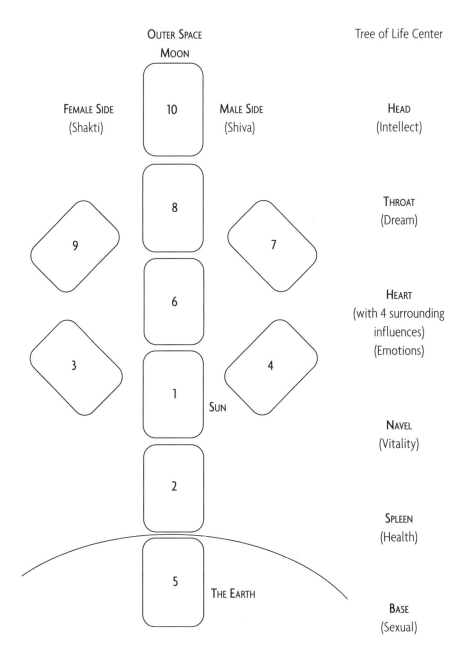

Figure 3. Tree of Life Chart

the sexual center and in an alchemical sense represents the base-material for bringing about the transformation.

Spleen or Digestive Center. The second of the cards is placed at the Spleen center, which represents the constitution of the questioner. This center is depicted as greenish, relating it to organic growth and in the middle is shown a mystic form known as Sri Yantra, consisting of nine interlaced triangles (the five upward-pointing triangles symbolizing the male principles), which itself represents the human body in an organic context. The number nine here relates to the truth of the universe within the body. The digestive force acts through this center, drawing up energy from the base and mixing it with the subtle vitalities of the Navel, so producing a kind of organic sap which sustains the Tree of Life and the subtle body. Eight subtle veins are depicted as greenish downward-moving tendrils of the tree, linking this place with the Earth. Cards falling at this location indicate health situations and medical diagnosis is implied here. This is the center of the organic life-rhythms. The card location here is the one which crosses the first card (present situation) and represents the opposing forces of good or evil.

Navel Center. The first of the cards is located at the Navel center, which is the place of transformation, the home of the Secret Dakinis. This indicates the situation surrounding the questioner of the Oracle, who can be imagined as sitting at this place, surrounded by the sixty-four cyclical influences of the dakinis, so bringing about a psychic transformation. The card-place is golden, with the form of the Great Illusion (Mahamaya) depicted seated and with many arms, symbolizing the many aspects of her form. This is the Solar Plexus of the physical body, the inner sun of the mystic. From here radiate sixty-four flames, these being understood as the Secret Dakini attendants of Mahamaya (the Great Illusion, representing the questioner). This is the place where all energies are refined, the alchemical vessel. As the "situation" of the questioner, it indicates what he or she consumes and how vitalities are gathered, and the degree of awareness of their functions and transformations. This center produces subtle vitalities which nourish the Spleen center and burn up materials such as food and subtle aggregates such as karma. It is also the attitude of the questioner, the Sun of our solar system.

Heart Center. The sixth of the cards is located at the Heart center, the root of all growth and psychic distillation, the all-encompassing power of love. It is the powerhouse, sending out the currents of life through the twenty-four major arteries, colored red, white and blue. Connecting the four emotive influences at this center, these arteries are like stems which surround it both contributing to and drawing from it. This is the center of emotion, symbolically colored black (indicating that it is unknowable in the ultimate sense), and taking the form of Mahakala, the great Time concept, the heart-beat, the extract of voidness in its creative potentiality. Outwardly this is expressed as the body of Kalachakra, the Time-Wheel, which has twenty-four veins, pumping out the essence of life to all the parts of the body. At this location the card indicates the influences coming in to the life of the questioner, the future.

The four influences on the heart are indicated as four card-places 3, 4, 7, 9, each of which has a black form with a different precious jewel. These four emotive influences are to be read as complementaries or oppositions, considering the symbolism on an intuitive level, and with particular regard to the elemental nature of the cards which fall there . . . the degrees of Fire, Water, Earth, etc. These four influences should be understood as joys in their exalted form, or poisons in the opposite.

Throat Center. The eighth of the cards is located at the Throat center, where the power of speech is centered. This place indicates the creative imagination, the world of fantasy and dreams. It is associated with the vibratory force holding all material objects together in their solid aspects. At this location the card indicates the environment (psychic or physical) which the questioner inhabits. The color for the card is light blue, symbolizing the all-pervading nature of imagination, and within is depicted the form of Vajrasattva, the peaceful manifestation of the guide or teacher in the aspect of the unity of Wisdom and Means. The sixteen veins of the subtle body of yoga are shown as moving upward as branches of the Tree of Life, these being the higher sublimation of the essence of the Heart. This place represents the wisdom and practice drawn from experience, understood particularly in the mystic sense with regard to the teacher, guide or example of an ideal.

Head Center. The tenth card is located at the Head center. This is the final outcome of the question put to the Oracle and is the resolution of the energies invoked and revealed through the previous cards. It is the extracted essence, the cooling "lunar drops" of nectar, the elixir of the fulfillment in the spiritual work. This card-position, or Psychic center, has thirty-two multi-colored rays emanating as the rainbow body of enlightenment. At this center is depicted the celestial Buddha Vajradhara, whose body is dark as outer space, and who is the holder of all indestructible things. He represents the highest aspirations of the Seeker and the resultant realization of fulfillment. He holds a sceptre and a bell, indicating that spiritual evolution is attained through the bringing together of Wisdom and Means outside of the realm of duality. This is the Lunar center of the intellect, from which the drops of wisdom flow, entering the other centers, particularly resting in the Heart.

The Tree of Life has its roots in the earth and its leaves reach out into space. The twin serpents intertwine while ascending the trunk of the Tree of Life, symbolizing the blending together of the male and female principles (yang/yin, shiva/shakti) in the process of spiritual and psychic integration. From the bowels of the earth,

The Tree of Life: The Subtle Body

depicted as a sphere of molten fire, the primordial energy ascends, transforming itself as it passes through the Psychic centers, through the Digestive center to the Transformation center at the Navel, where the sixty-four dakini wisdom-energies dance, to the Heart center, Throat center and ultimately to the crown of the Head center, within which is the cooling lunar force of the intellect. An inner subtle distillation takes place, precipitating as wisdom resting in the Heart and distributed to all the parts of the being. The tantric cosmology, weaving inner and outer worlds, is beautifully evoked by this chart of the Tree of Life and makes a potent ground to relate to *The Tantric Dakini Oracle* cards as an oracle. As a meditation chart, with or without individual cards laid upon it, the Tree of Life is a source of spiritual inspiration.

Method of The Great Universe Map

The Tantric Dakini Oracle cards may be laid out directly on The Great Universe Map in order to obtain an astrological picture of the consultation (to order the Great Universe Map, see page 207). After the cards have been well shuffled and cut nine times, the first card in the pack is turned over and laid in the place of Aries (No. 1 in Figure 4), the first house. Then the other cards are turned over, one at a time, and placed in the zodiacal houses on the places indicated on the chart, starting with Taurus and Gemini and on through to Pisces in the twelfth house. Interpretation of the cards should be made according to standard astrological procedures. The thirteenth card is placed at the center, representing the questioner and the resolution of the question, according to the card located there. The consultation of *The Tantric Dakini Oracle* with regard to the Map of the Great Universe is of particular value for determining psychological readings relating to personality types.

TABLE 1. DAKINI CARD LOCATION AND ASTROLOGICAL HOUSES

Card Order on Chart	Astrological Sign	Meaning (Traditional Astrology)
1	Aries	Personality, Appearance of the Questioner, Outlook and Potential.
2	Taurus	Material Possessions, Finance, Stability related to the Earth.
3	Gemini	Communication, Letters, Journeys, Mental Action.
4	Cancer	Home Environment, Old Age, the Parents, the End of Life.
5	Leo	Heart, Love Affairs, Children, Speculations, Exciting Innovations, Leadership.
6	Virgo	Health and Work, Food, either physical or spiritual.
7	Libra	Marriage, Partnerships, Dealings with the Public, Balance.
8	Scorpio	The Occult, Sexual Experience, Ruler of Death, Money.
9	Sagittarius	Law, Philosophy, the Dream World, Ideals.
10	Capricorn	Profession, Accomplishment, Fame, the Provider, the Mother.
11	Aquarius	Hopes, Wishes, Aspirations, Intellectual Ideals, Friends.
12	Pisces	Faculties, Restrictive Limitations, Karma, Secret Enemies, Strengths or Weaknesses.
13	The Questioner/ The Question	

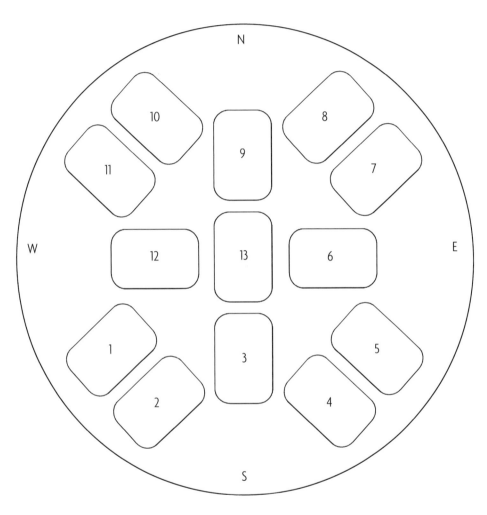

Figure 4. Great Universe Map

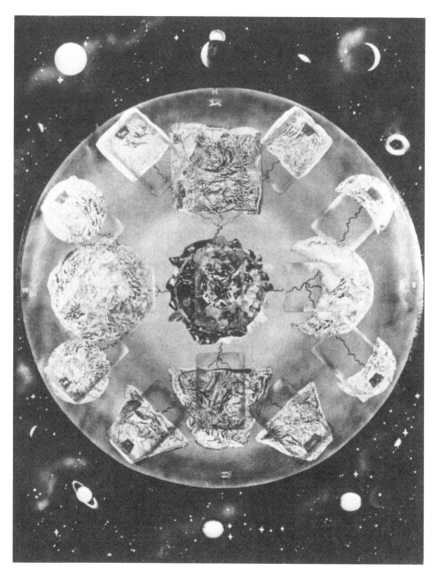

The Great Universe: An Astrological Map

Composition of the Oracle

Once the Oracle cards have been laid out it will be helpful to read the description of the symbolism and the divinatory meaning.

The cards which relate to the Major Arcana of the Tarot (0-21) have particularly potent divinatory meanings. We have given variant readings for different locations in some instances; otherwise, the general divinatory meaning applies.

Cards related to the Suits of the Minor Arcana (22-61) change their specific divinatory meanings more frequently, according to their location on the Tree of Life chart.

Time cards (62-64) are not found in the Tarot. In *The Tantric Dakini Oracle* system they offer possibilities for directly resolving the influences of destiny. Helpful indications are given.

All interpretations and divinatory meanings are guidelines only. As the reader becomes familiar with the cards and their symbolism, the different relationships will become clearer. *The Tantric Dakini Oracle* cards are most effective on an intuitive level. Spontaneous interpretation through an awareness of tantric symbolism is both direct and personal.

The cards may be successfully consulted for a person in his absence by bearing that person in mind at the time of shuffling and dealing.

There are no reverse card readings, as in the Tarot. Dakini cards are placed directly in position, right way up.

The Tantric Dakini Oracle cards are comprised of:

- A card conceived of as the center of a cycle of transformation, taking the form of a JOKER, around which the psychological energies move in the play of life. The number of the joker is zero.
- Sixty-four cyclical cards, representing the energies of transformation moving conceptually around a fixed joker. These cards are divided up in the following way:

1–21	Card-images related to the Major Arcana of the traditional Tarot.
22–31	Card-images related to the Minor Arcana of the traditional Tarot, of the element "Air" and the suit of Swords.
32–41	Card-images related to the Minor Arcana of the traditional Tarot, of the element "Fire" and the suit of Wands.
42–51	Card-images related to the Minor Arcana of the traditional Tarot, of the element "Water" and the suit of Cups.
52–61	Card-images related to the Minor Arcana of the traditional Tarot, of the element "Earth" and the suit of Pentacles.
62	The Past
63	The Present
64	The Future

The Numerology of the Cards

The Tantric Dakini Oracle cards are numbered from 0 through 64. Their numerology has particular significance and aids the rapid interpretation of specific situations or readings.

Use the traditional numerological method of adding up the numbers of all the cards in a given reading and reducing the grand total to a double or single figure by again adding together the digits. Pocket calculators are of practical assistance. Numerology can be used to determine precise influences bearing on a reading.

All the cards of The Tantric Dakini Oracle add up to the number 2080, which in turn reduces to 2 + 8, equivalent to the number 10. Card number 10 is the WHEEL OF GREAT TIME, on which the cycle of The Tantric Dakini Oracle is based. A further reduction gives the single digit "1," the number of the Magician of the traditional Tarot or the MERCURY card of our deck.

All readings can be dealt with in such a manner, by adding up the numbers and reducing them to basics. Fuller elaboration of numerological methods will be found in the sample readings at the back of the book.

Different Methods of Reading

There are many different ways of using the cards apart from the standard Celtic Cross, Tree of Life or Great Universe types of readings. The choice really lies with the diviner, who may use any system with which he or she is familiar. In addition, the cards can be used as meditation devices, telepathic targets, or for guessing games and many other activities. Games can be invented spontaneously, collecting related elements, archetypes or symbolic concepts.

PART II:

Brief Meanings
of Individual Cards

THE NUMBERING AND BRIEF MEANING OF THE TANTRIC DAKINI CARDS

MAJOR ARCANA

No.	Dakini Title	Brief Meaning	Tarot Relationship
0	Joker	Humor in all situations, the center of the pack, the point of transformation.	Fool
1	Mercury	Spiritual fulfillment, the creative intellect, the power of the Will to transform situations.	Magician
2	Isis: The High Priestess	The occult path, a boon card of intuition, attainment of wishes.	High Priestess
3	Scarlet Woman	The female mystic Energy, passion, an affair of the heart or of the Occult Tantric Path.	Empress
4	Hot Seat	Position of responsibility, a potent position, decisions to be made, balance.	Emperor
5	Ganesh: Lord of Obstacles	Obstacles to be overcome through confrontation, transformatory success.	Hierophant
6	Wish-Fulfilling Gem	The fulfillment of a wish, a mystic experience, spiritual evolution, the heart.	Lovers
7	Cremation Ground/ Meditation	The transient nature of all things, spiritual rebirth, visualization.	Chariot

#	Card	Meaning	Traditional
8	Living Goddess	The earthly manifestation of spirituality, duty toward higher ideals, self-development.	Justice
9	Way Through	The key of the self, auspiciousness, a way through to overcome problems, attainment.	Hermit
10	Wheel of Great Time	Burning up Karmas, completion of the cycle of destiny, success through action.	Wheel of Fortune
11	Self-Created	Self-reliance, inner resources and the power of faith, a Heart card, highly auspicious.	Strength
12	Slay the Ego	Fruition, cutting through bonds of the ego, the breaking of habits, self-surrendering.	Hanged Man
13	Death/Transfiguration	Occult transfiguration, regeneration, the removal of fears through Tantric confrontation.	Death
14	Puja/Purification	Mental foundations, absolution, the purification of the self, dedication, humility, the spiritual Path.	Temperence
15	Ally	The overcoming of lower orders of consciousness, the guardian of the inner self, the power of the unconscious.	Devil
16	Holocaust	Spiritual victory, dramatic action, change, the loss of one thing in order to gain another.	Tower
17	Island of Jewels	The realization of hopes and aspirations, inspiration and insight, spiritual possibilities.	Star

No.	Dakini Title	Brief Meaning	Tarot Relationship
18	Soma	The entry of forces of fulfillment, higher initiation, the intuition and imagination, wisdom, ascent of the psyche.	Moon
19	Phoenix	Mystical attainment, rebirth, selfless love, an affair, marriage, the alchemical fire of transformation.	Sun
20	Transformation	Auspiciousness, self-development through psychic transformation, the Spirit supreme over matter.	Judgment
21	Earthbound	The meaning of existence, development, completion of a cycle, action as the result of choice, free will.	World
		MINOR ARCANA	
22	Mother's Milk	Spiritual homesickness, the desire to return to the source of all things, aspiration for non-duality.	Air
23	Maya: How She Spins	The transient nature of all things, the Great Illusion, control of fate, a possible emotional threat.	Air
24	Solar Return	Returns to the roots of personality, astrological influences, overcoming of obstacles through recognition.	Air
25	Threefold Riddle	The riddle card, psychological temptation, discrimination required, deep personal meaning, change of residence, development.	Air

26	Mean and Heavy	Evolutionary responsibility, fearlessness, preparation to overcome difficulties, practical position, ruthless.	Air
27	Magic Carpet	Positive influence of the occult, influence of forces, transport and delight, change of residence, development.	Air
28	Cosmic Carrot	The occult transmission, earnest desire for liberation, discipline, commitment to the spiritual path, fruition.	Air
29	Self-Preservation	Integrity, withdrawal into the self in order to preserve one's position, a timeless wisdom-aspect of eternity.	Air
30	Castles in the Clouds	Higher development of the Will, vivid imagination, but a need to achieve creative fulfillment, positive direction.	Air
31	Just Passing Through	Recognition of principles of trinity and unity as being a fundamental truth, a psychological stance, a view of reality.	Air
32	Shiva: The Pillar of Fire	The astral light, spiritual fulfillment of a high order, the Head center, Illumination, mystic revelation.	Fire
33	Eternal Life	Mystic completion, the eternal resting place of the psyche, the solution of a problem, clarity, reincarnation/rebirth understood.	Fire
34	Burning Bush/ Lineage Tree	Completion of occult preparation, opportunity, and direct contact with spirituality, insight, revelation, faith.	Fire
35	As Above/So Below	Resolution of complementaries, card of the Heart, the refinement of the emotions, the truth of alchemy, good fortune.	Fire

No.	Dakini Title	Brief Meaning	Tarot Relationship
36	Guardian	Entry into higher tantric initiations, potent protection, the burning up of all illusory concepts, firm roots on the spiritual path, the guide.	Fire
37	Fire of Sacrifice	Consciousness through sacrifice, commitment, deliberate act of self-sacrifice, development of faith through action.	Fire
38	A-Musement	The female power-principle channeled, pleasure and occult fulfillment, the integration of the sensual with the spiritual, letting go.	Fire
39	Serpent Power	The power at the root of mystic transformation, the pure energy of sexuality, evolutionary change, creativity, power, achievement.	Fire
40	Blow Your Mind	Completion leading to sudden spiritual release, a change of viewpoint, get rid of habits, a new dimension of spontaneous action.	Fire
41	High Tension	Physical power channeled by the Will, the position of the warrior, the outpouring of energy to maintain one's situation, high tension.	Fire
42	Wave of Bliss	Harmony as an attribute of wisdom, resolution, consummation, the path of ecstasy, rebirth of the psyche, dissolution of dualities.	Water
43	Mount Meru: Center of the Universe	The integration of inner and outer worlds, the spiritual path, revaluation, firm will, upliftment.	Water
44	Heart Drop	Initiation into the higher aspect of the self, an alchemical concept of personality distillation, the mystic vision, wisdom of the heart.	Water

#	Card	Meaning	Element
45	Like a Bubble	The path of the self as related to the world, the release of all preconceptions, opening of the mind, the spontaneous nature	Water
46	Abundance	Fulfillment of the self in harmony with the world, a fortunate change of circumstance, material abundance, money, spirituality.	Water
47	Horseplay	The occult path of spontaneity, the imagination, the clear entry into the world of fantasy, a transcendent experience, sexual moment.	Water
48	White Lady: Mother of Pearl	The projected self in a position of power, weakness of commitment, morbidity, detachment, the analytical mind.	Water
49	Cutting Through	The resolution of the path of the self, decisive action in all areas, practicality, real action to do with destiny, change.	Water
50	Recall/Memory	The path of the unconscious as initiation, recollect, memory of the past, emotional longings, recall all experiences, act.	Water
51	Deep End	The path of the self related to psyche evolution, abandoning of restrictions made by the ego, adaptation, unconscious motivations.	Water
52	The Rose Garden	Fulfillment of the path of intuition, the heightening of the senses, mystical sensuality, luxury, abundance, creativity.	Earth
53	Tree Spirit: Yakshi	The power path of Nature, solution to a problem, understanding of natural cycles of forces, growth, elementals accepted.	Earth
54	Asylum	The path of balance as an attribute of initiation, refuge and real recuperation, freedom from worldly concerns, a mystic position, positive omen.	Earth

No.	Dakini Title	Brief Meaning	Tarot Relationship
55	Totally Bananas	The path of psychic release, freed latent energies, an unconscious fantasy, the ridiculous in all things, unconventionality.	Earth
56	Elixir Fruit/Essence	The path of the exalted senses, the taste of all worldly things, fertile ground for growth, distillation, discrimination.	Earth
57	Temptation	The path of occult choice, a tempting offer, a decision to be made, psychological turning point, doorway through to the occult.	Earth
58	Chameleon	The path of adaptability, change to suit the environment, the need to take a firm position, fickleness, ability for fantasy, change.	Earth
59	Pearls Before Swine	The path of discrimination through self-awareness, guard against disillusionment, disappointments, choice of company kept.	Earth
60	Taking Up Arms	The acceptance of responsibility as an expression of evolution, fearlessness, position of strength, self-discipline, invulnerability.	Earth
61	Survival	Unity within the self as related to the world, instinct to survive despite all obstacles, pollution of the world or of the psyche, power of faith.	Earth

TIME CARDS

No.	Dakini Title	Brief Meaning	Tarot Relationship
62	Dangerous Pussy/The Past	The potent power of the past, the protector of all the dakinis, the occult tantric transmission, initiation into gnosis, action.	
63	Centering/The Present	The potent power of the present, the inner and outer as one unit of strength, the eternal present, desires achieved, truth.	
64	The Last Laugh/The Future	The potent power of the future, the exalted cycle of transformation, freedom from Karma through humor, advantage gained.	

PART III:

The Tantric Dakini Oracle

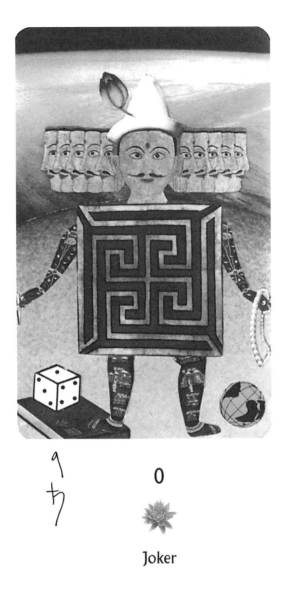

0

Joker

JOKER bears the number "0," signifying the voidness from which all things emerge and into which every creation dissolves, and occupies the central position around which the 64 Secret Dakinis dance in the play of life. He is related to the Fool of the traditional Tarot, but his attributes are more cosmic; he does not carry the idea of immaturity and folly but is the enlightened player of the game of life.

The joker is depicted standing on the orb of the sun, his back to the earth as viewed from space. He is in the form of Brahma the Creator, with eleven heads signifying the unity of all things; he wears the traditional dunce's hat, ornamented with a lotus blossom, the symbol of spiritual enlightenment. The body of the joker is composed of a double swastika symbol, meaning that positivity and negativity are combined in him as non-duality, pointing to his cosmic function as movement in both directions.

His right hand holds a pen, showing that he is the writer of destiny, the maker of the Akashic Records wherein all accounts of the past, present, and future are stored. The left hand holds a pearl rosary, indicating his concern that the links in the chain of destiny be maintained. The rest of his body is cosmic, bearing auspicious symbols and containing all worlds. His right foot rests on a volume of the I-Ching, the Chinese Book of Changes, upon which is a dice bearing the number of Saturn, showing that he rules over fate and destiny. His left foot playfully kicks the ball of the world.

Divinatory Meaning

The importance of maintaining humor in all situations, as a hot-line to understanding all situations of life. Do not get caught up in concepts of inevitability or destiny but realize that all situations are but jokes of Brahma as the joker. Become the joker and accept the humor of situations. The gaining of ascendancy. Always a positive interpretation.

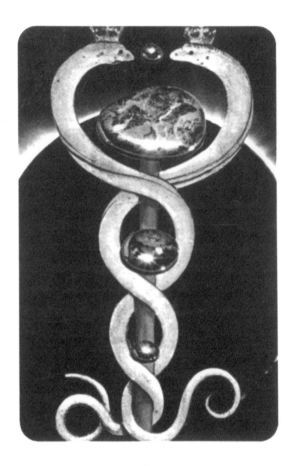

1

Mercury

MERCURY bears the number "1," signifying the truth of unity and invoking the concepts of masculinity as an active function related to the creative intellect. This card has some affinity with the Magician of the Tarot.

Two serpents are shown entwined around a central staff, a wand of Mercury, the whole forming the mystic caduceus, the symbol of magical transformation. The snakes wind around the staff three and one-half times, likening them to the coiled kundalini serpent-energy emanating from the Base or sexual center. The staff symbolizes the spinal column, through which the raw serpent-energy travels and is transformed. The aim of awakening the kundalini-energy is to pass the most potent inner forces upward, piercing and illuminating the inner psychic centers (the chakras), resulting in drops of wisdom distilled in the region of the Head, the seat of the higher intellect. This card represents the primordial energy (the inner shakti) transformed alchemically into an elixir, depicted as fluid mercury and harnessed as four stable pools. These are related to the main psychic centers of the subtle body, at the Navel, Heart, Throat and Head regions.

This is a symbol of the realization and fulfillment stage of tantric practice, as is suggested by the crowns on the heads of the snakes. The background reveals itself as a black sun, indicating the mystery of energy transformed into something beyond our worldly concepts. Mercury in its raw stage is a poison, but if used correctly it can produce gold. This alchemical concept here takes on a psychological meaning: the gold of spirituality and enlightenment.

Divinatory Meaning

Spiritual fulfillment, enlightenment, distillation, sudden moments of deep realization. The creative intellect exalted. Indicating that all experiences (both positive and negative) should be known and experienced within the subtle body of transformation. Self-control, utilized to achieve ultimate perfection and spiritual goals. The transforming power of the Will, the intentional act. In the Spleen center this indicates a possible danger to health. Otherwise it is always very positive. Meditate on the form of the subtle or transformation body.

2

Isis: The High Priestess

ISIS: THE HIGH PRIESTESS bears the number "2," signifying the truth of complementary opposites united and implying a blending of emotion and intuition as an exalted feminity wisdom-archetype. She is related to the High Priestess of the Tarot.

The head and shoulders of Isis, who is also known as Ishtar the High Priestess, are seen as if rising through a nebulous veil of a night sky. She is considered to be guarding the doorway through to occult knowledge. Her position is that of a wisdom-holder *(prajnadhari)*, an attendant and guardian of the great Secret Dakini realm. An initiatress.

The night-sky symbolizes the limitless nature and awe inspiring qualities of her territory, the wisdom which she guards so carefully. Traditionally this wisdom is never revealed to the uninitiated and therefore this aspect of Isis is portrayed showing only her bared head and shoulders. It is said that, like the sleeping Venus, if her full nakedness or potency is exposed prematurely, without adequate psychic preparation, there is a chance that the occult mysteries revealed through her might be misunderstood or abused. Her two eyes are rubies, indicating her fire-like inner nature, and on her forehead is an open third eye which points to her function as a distiller of arcane knowledge and tells of deep intuitive penetration. She wears ornaments indicating her exalted position. On her head are two golden horns forming the shape of an upturned crescent moon. The archetype of Isis, the High Priestess, is here depicted as an anima-glyph.

Divinatory Meaning

Serious intention to find the meaning behind all phenomena. The intention to dedicate oneself to the search for enlightenment and a deep interest in the occult. This is a boon card, a blessing, a guardian angel showing the intuitive path through to the mysteries. Isis is related to the dark aspect of the moon, to the astrological sign Scorpio, to gnosis, to the cycles of Nature, indicating attainment of wishes and particularly of spiritual fulfillment. Meditate upon her as a wondrous and beautiful galaxy which guards many deep secrets.

- intiatrix
- red ruby eyes
Isis - dark moon - ♏

3

Scarlet Woman

SCARLET WOMAN bears the number "3," signifying the threefold nature of existence (as Creation, Preservation and Dissolution), the trinity, the trine of astrology, the Past, Present and Future, the three-fold cycle of destiny. This card has some affinity with the Empress of the Tarot.

The two large eyes of the Scarlet Woman as a goddess stare out over a cluster of small red flowers. In the foreground there is a large open red poppy, relating her to the earth in its fruitfulness and fecundity. She represents the threefold play of the goddess, the shakti, in her sensual and sexual aspects through her magnetic form. She is the seductive yogini (female aspect of yoga-fulfillment) of the left-hand tantric path, which stresses that there should be no hesitation to perform potent acts provided one is prepared to handle the consequences.

The red color indicates the sulphurous nature of her energy, as the raw female principle in the alchemical process of self-realization. The open poppy indicates that the womb of the goddess is open in a mystic invitation. On her brow is depicted a ruby, related to her fire-like transcendental nature, at the same time pointing out that, so sure is she of her position of authority, she wears her potency as ornaments.

Divinatory Meaning

This card indicates the importance of the shakti or female energy principle to the questioner, and her manifestation either as the mystic counterpart in the world or as the attainment of her attributes within the self. It suggests a strongly passionate nature, from the sensual to the spiritual realms, either latent or expressed in the heart of the questioner. This is very much a Heart card, representing the resolution of divisions between spiritual and material, indicating the wondrous creative fulfillment to be achieved through coming to terms with her archetype. She is also to be related to the Base or sexual center, a location therein possibly indicating an affair or even a pregnancy. Meditate on her as the creative female principle.

4

Hot Seat

HOT SEAT bears the number "4," signifying the deeper self rooted in firm foundations and convictions, it is the even number of balance, the four pillars of the universe, the four directions. This card has some affinity with the Emperor of the Tarot.

A fine carved wooden throne is depicted situated out in space, surrounded by solar flares and balls of fire. The throne itself has a base of carved lions, symbolizing the enormous power of any person sitting on this exalted place. It is a position of great responsibility.

From the seat of the throne great flames issue forth, indicating the tremendous masculine transforming power inherent here. This power is related to spiritual and secular authority. The seat is that of a master of the Universe; any person prepared to take such a position should first be sure that adequate work has been achieved and that he or she is prepared for responsibility. Under the seat is depicted the mystic Stone of Scone, over which many battles have been fought and many lives lost. Here it is still only a stone, though it has a practical function as a support once the flames have been overcome.

Divinatory Meaning

This card indicates being put on the spot, that a position of authority, or responsibility has been thrust upon the questioner and that he or she is obliged to make themselves equal to it. This is a position of great urgency, where decisions have to be made, demanding inner conviction and powers of leadership. It tells of a way through to the realization of ambitions, particularly those relating to authority and power. In the Base center it indicates a fortification of the raw energy of transformation, leading to fulfillment. In the Spleen center it relates to the fire of digestion; in the Heart, to commitment through the acceptance of responsibility. Meditate on the correct channeling of energy through the higher Will, transforming and blending the psyche.

5

Ganesh: Lord of Obstacles

GANESH: LORD OF OBSTACLES bears the number "5," signifying organization and the pathway through all obstacles. This relates to ordered centering in the world and the entry through to the inner mandala, the mystic circle of psychic protection. The card has some affinity with the Hierophant of the Tarot.

Ganesh is a Hindu god with the head of an elephant and the body of a man. He is shown seated in his exalted form in the middle of a spider's web. He has four hands which symbolize the earth quality of the psychic center over which he rules, the Base region of the subtle body. He holds an axe, indicating that he is a hero, and wears an elaborate crown and ornaments. It is Ganesh who is always invoked at the beginning of all Hindu rites. His name is invoked to help overcome all obstacles. His nature is compassionate and he represents both knowledge and wealth. The spider's web is the symbol of *maya* (the Illusion), the warp and weft of all relative (as opposed to absolute) existence. Here, in place of a spider, Ganesh is shown, for he helps to overcome rather than to be trapped by *maya*, the Illusion.

Divinatory Meaning

This card suggests that there are obstacles to be overcome. The only way to get through the obstacles of the spider's web of the world and its illusory aspects is to become a lord of these obstacles. This can only be done by confronting these things, to the point where one sees through them, so to eliminate the cause behind the effect. If this is achieved, either through penetration or through surrendering, then one becomes lord of the three worlds, rather than caught in them, so achieving the respect which this position merits. What must be borne in mind is the necessity to begin at the Base, to recognize evolutionary order, to gain ascendancy and to remember through personalized ritual. Ganesh is an occult "Ally," a helper. At the Base center this card represents strength and is a positive location. At the Spleen center it could indicate a health hazard. In the Navel center it suggests transformatory success (either monetary, since Ganesh is Lord of Money, or psychological); in the Heart center, either an emotional obstacle (in the world) or mystic opening through devotion (out of the world). Meditate on the web of Illusion, placing oneself at the center as an omniscient lord.

6

Wish-Fulfilling Gem

WISH-FULFILLING GEM bears the number "6," signifying harmony, the balanced blend of intellect and emotion, the Head and the Heart. It is the number of the sixth sense and the entry into the world of fulfillment. Relates to the Lovers of the Tarot.

From the tranquil lake of bottomless quietude the Wish-fulfilling Gem rises up. Within its multifaceted form the All-Good Buddha

Samantabhadra and his female counterpart Samantabhadri are seated. In this male/female tantric aspect they represent the non-dual perfect Buddhahood of peaceful compassion. The emanations from this mystic form are like the rainbow hues of the white light refracted from the facets of a diamond. The glyph is crowned with a smaller version of itself, which is reflected in the water below. The whole forms a double mystic scepter *(vajra)*, suggesting the unlimited nature of this essence principle as projected on the mind-sky of inner space. This card depicts divine love in its most sacred and benign aspect, the resolution of all dualities.

Divinatory Meaning

This card is the most potent boon card of the deck. It may always be interpreted as the fulfillment of a wish, though the emphasis is on the mystic rather than the worldly. On the lowest level it may be just good luck, and on the spiritual level (in the Heart or Head) it indicates deep metaphysical development, maturation and the fruit of endeavor. Much can be gained from concentrated meditation on this card, the father and mother of all Buddhas. Imagine the light within the jewel of the self, and then place oneself within. Visualize the effulgent emanations of light. Feel the compassionate essence. In the chart of the Tree of Life as a subtle body, the mystic form of the All-Good Buddha and his consort is depicted above the moon of the Head center, since this is the traditional location according to tantra. This indicates the evolutionary archetypal ancestor of the human spirit, to which we must all ultimately return. The card tells of spiritual guidance and ultimate realization. It indicates a "coming into balance and harmony."

7

Cremation Ground / Meditation

CREMATION GROUND/MEDITATION bears the number "7," signifying the law of seven, the occult path and the mystical perfection achieved through becoming one with this principle. It is the number of the octave, the recurring natural harmonic to which all worlds and elements are subject. The Chariot of the Tarot has some affinity with this card.

The foreground is littered with human skulls and bones, reminding us of the transient nature of life on earth. In India the cremation grounds are considered places of great potency, where yogis can remain undisturbed to practice their meditation. The proximity of corpses and bones is believed to act as a powerful reminder of the need to achieve detachment from the world, so enhancing the desire for enlightenment. All worldly things ultimately must become part of the great cremation ground and it is the recognition of this fundamental truth which benefits the yogi or meditator.

In the black night sky behind the cremation ground, the orb of the earth is seen rising, showing that this scene of the end of the world is to be understood as a revelation through which the earth and life is reborn. Reality is here being transmuted into surreality. The end of one period and the beginning of a new perspective.

Divinatory Meaning

Develop the faculty of visualization and meditate on the transient nature of all things connected with this world. In doing so, you will gain power from this concept and it will become a ground of reference for all action. This card suggests a spiritual rebirth, but this can only be achieved through the development of concentration, so that the inner eye will be able to see through all material phenomena. Courage and fortitude are needed, but the implication is that ascendancy is within reach, perhaps even already achieved. The location of this card at different psychic centers in the Tree of Life chart is of great significance to understanding the meaning. At the Throat it suggests mystic visionary revelation; in the Heart, the need for detachment; and at the Navel, a change of perspective.

8

Living Goddess

LIVING GODDESS bears the number "8," signifying perfect balance through positive channeling of power, culminating in spiritual evolution. It is the number of the planet Saturn, who in occult traditions is the power-principle upholding the equilibrium of creation. This card relates to Justice of the Tarot.

A beautiful young woman looks down from an arched window

in space, a view of the earth clearly visible below. She is the Living Goddess, known in India and Nepal as Kumari, who, for the duration of her appointment, symbolizes the untainted virgin-essence, the divine energy of femininity incarnate (the *adi-shakti*). She is the personification of the virgin goddess, one of the eight major goddesses of the Hindu Pantheon. After her selection by oracle, she appears before the public at her traditional temple in Kathmandu. The sight of her is said to bring good luck and prosperity.

The Living Goddess is adorned with jewels and on her forehead wears the mask of vermilion, indicating her divine origin. She wears costly robes of red and gold, symbolic of her exalted spiritual nature.

Divinatory Meaning

The earthly manifestation of spiritual qualities, the concept of being chosen, and a sense of duty toward higher ideals. An evolved self-development to meet a position which one has been put in, either in the world or out of it. Indicates the potency of the miraculous, and an evolved aesthetical position of reference. This card is particularly positive in the spiritual sense, suggesting compassion and resignation. At the Heart center it means fulfillment; in the Head, the mystic acceptance of divine principles. It is a guardian card, related to the astrological signs Libra and Aquarius, indicating equilibrium and balance of an occult nature.

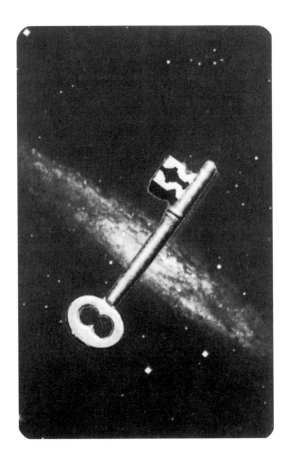

9

Way Through

WAY THROUGH bears the number "9," signifying the completion of one cycle and the beginning of another. It is an occult number, the ennead, the number of the microcosm, indicating psychic resolution and the ability to find a way through to other dimensions. This card relates to the Hermit of the Tarot.

A great key is depicted across a swirling galaxy of stars in the limitless night-sky of the universe. This is a cosmic key which opens up the Akashic Records wherein all accounts of destiny, past, present, and future, are forever stored. This key opens the door to both arcne and worldly wisdom, depending on its location on the chart. In the worldly places it may represent the solution of a problem, particularly related to karma.

Divinatory Meaning

The self contains all things, as the microcosm to the macrocosm, and it is within the self that the key is located. This is a highly auspicious card, suggesting that the questioner is really involved in the search for truth. It indicates the resolution of a problem, the receiving of occult teaching, spiritual guidance and the attainment of goals. At all positions in the Tree of Life chart, the interpretation is resolution. With this key do not hesitate to act.

10

Wheel of Great Time

WHEEL OF GREAT TIME bears the number "10," signifying the completion of a cycle of time. It is the coming together of the digits "1" (the unity) with "0," the voidness from which all things emerge and into which all things dissolve. The number "10" is a completion. It relates to the Wheel of Fortune of the Tarot.

In the center of a clock face the form of Mahakali (the Great

Mother of Time) is depicted in divine union with her consort Shiva
Mahakala (the Great Ruler of Time). In one hand she holds a
sword, symbolizing her function as the power (shakti) which cuts
through the past, present and future. Her other two hands hold a
skull-bowl filled with blood, symbolizing the integration of renunciation and compassion. She has three arms, indicating that she rules
over the three times. The fire tells of the burning up of past karma
in the completion of activity, the burning and transforming of destiny itself. The eyes and skulls around the clock face denote that
Mahakali rules over the cycles of lives beyond death, and that she is
the guardian of the Great Time Wheel, which includes but is not
limited to temporal and linear time structures. The eye at the center is the all-seeing eye of the Egyptian god Horus, reminding us
that there is a constant unchanging center to all changing phenomena. Two eyes take fluid form at the base of the circle, representing
the fluidity and mutability of the world of fate and fortune.

Divinatory Meaning

All things are ever-changing, in a state of flux, yet there are cycles of
such activity. Do not let yourself be caught up on the circumference
of situations but concentrate on the center. Burn up past karmas by
decisive right action, so becoming the ruler of the present and the
future. This card indicates success through the completion of a
time-cycle, an unexpected change of luck for the better. Depending
on the location in the Tree of Life it is either concerned with the
world or with influences from outside. By meditating on the Wheel
of Great Time one can bring fate back into one's own hands, will-
ing the course of destiny.

11

Self-Created

SELF-CREATED bears the number "11," signifying the integration of unity as recognition of the principle of self-creation. It is a new beginning, related to the eleven year cycle of the sun. It has some affinity with the Strength card of the traditional Tarot, through this card has a more mystic indication.

On a still blue lake covered with lotus leaves a large pink lotus occupies a central position in the foreground. Two hands are shown as emerging from the center of this lotus, with joined palms upward, cradling and exhibiting a naked flame of pink and blue. The flame represents original creativity within the petals of self-made spiritual enfoldment, symbolized by the lotus. The lake is the ground of all becoming, the leaves represent the multiple possibilities of manifestations on the surface of reality. The drops of dew are as wisdom-drops, the higher distillations of the psyche. In the tantric tradition there was once a great teacher known as Padmasambhava, meaning "self-created from a lotus," who was a second Buddha. He transmitted the tantric teachings to Tibet from India. This card invokes a powerful memory of mystic strength leading to spiritual unfoldment.

Divinatory Meaning

Self-reliance. All creativity can be found within the self, manifested as a seed which can become a blossom. The heart can produce from within itself everything needed for realizing one's goals. This is a very favorable card, suggesting great inner resources and the power of faith over material ambition in the process of self-realization and in bringing ideals into the world. It is, in particular, a Heart card, a location therein on the Tree of Life would indicate a magnitude of spiritual development. At other locations it tells of specific degrees of spirituality. It is a symbol of the triumph of love and its power in the spiritual realms.

12

Slay the Ego

SLAY THE EGO bears the number "12," signifying fruition, the blending of complementaries as a complete expression devoid of all ego. It relates to the Hanged Man of the traditional Tarot, though this aspect here depicted is less to do with the world and more concerned with the psyche and its place in the cosmos.

Way out in limitless space the goddess Kali is depicted against a milky nebula, her dark body reminding us of the vastness of outer space. She is known as Kalaratri, the "Night of Destruction," the event which will happen at the end of the world, and which is necessary before a new world can be created. She has four arms, holding a sword with which to slay the ego, the head of a demon killed by her in battle, and the last two in mystic gestures indicating that she grants boons and rids her devotees of all fears. She is seated in the lotus posture of equilibrium, wears a crown, and is garlanded with severed heads (symbolizing the original matrix-vibrations comprising all material things). Her tongue is extended and red, indicating her all-consuming nature. She is not bound by any earthly restrictions and her function is to help cut through these kinds of bondage. As the "Destroyer of Time" she is the "Slayer of the Ego," which is depicted by the decapitated head of the demon, which she holds by the hair.

Divinatory Meaning

Forsake the particularization of self for participation in the universal dance of life. Dissolve the veil which separates the self from the one divine unity. With courage and insight cut through the bondage of the ego. Renounce all that impedes progress, break with habits and habit-forming thoughts. Self-surrender, leading to personality transformation. Interpretation of the meaning of this card depends much on its location in the Tree of Life chart. At the Base center it concerns the world; in the Spleen the indication is habits of food and assimilation; in the Navel center, the psychological stance. Meditate on dark Kali as both destroyer and regenerator, cutting away all that needs to be shed.

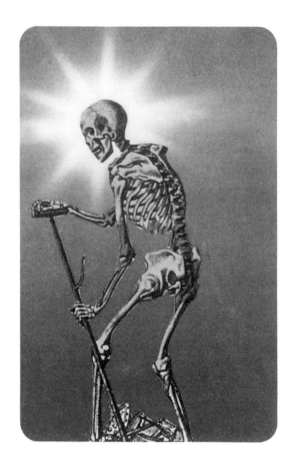

13

Death / Transfiguration

DEATH/TRANSFIGURATION bears the number "13," the combination of "1" the Unity and "3" the Trinity, indicating the perpetuity of the creative movement, and the position at the center of all time cycles. It is also the number of superstition, the key to the occult transfiguration. Related to Death of the Tarot.

The card depicts a skeleton in the traditional pose of Death the

THE TANTRIC DAKINI ORACLE 63

Reaper. In this card he holds a staff instead of a scythe, symbolizing the spinal column on which the psychic centers or chakras are threaded. The branch sprouting from the staff suggests the organic life still present and indicates the possibility of regeneration. Cosmic white light emanates from behind the head of the skeleton, showing that death, the loss of the physical temple of the body, is but a step nearer the pure light of consciousness. The card depicts the transcendant spirit, freed from the body, renewed and reborn. Beneath the feet of Death are represented the things of the world, abandoned.

Divinatory Meaning

The end of things as previously known. The breaking of ties, the death of the old self paving the way for regeneration and enlightenment. The removal of fears through confrontation. The awakening of spiritual awareness, possibly through a traumatic event such as illness or through an inner realization. The reconciliation of opposites. Abstraction or a state of inertia needing a change of outlook. Death as the door to the beyond, the post-death states, a *bardo* or intermediary psychological condition. Change, through transfiguration and the realization of new opportunities. Interpretation of the meaning of this card depends much on its location at different centers in the Tree of Life chart. At the Base it concerns the world; in the Spleen the indication is danger to health; possibly a change of attitude due to death of a friend; in the Throat, the mystical position; in the Head, the outcome of the question. Meditate on this card as an initiation, as a guardian.

14

Puja / Purification

PUJA/PURIFICATION bears the number "14," a highly charged occult number signifying mental foundation and the completion of a cosmic creative cycle of seven an octave of illuminating intelligence-principle. This card is related to the Temperance card of the traditional Tarot.

A priest is shown pouring water onto a black stone lingam

(phallus) set within a square pool. This is the shiva lingam, the phallus representing the male energy of Shiva, in the famous Golden Temple of Vishvanath (Lord of the Universe) in Benares, India. The devotee-priest is performing *puja* (an act of worship) by pouring consecrated water over the stone, representative of the male cosmic principle. In this act the Lord of the Universe is honored and this same principle is contacted within the self. The intention and result of this action is depicted by the shower of flowers, seen either as a cascade descending from above, or as a whirling column ascending to the source. The pouring thus acts in two dimensions simultaneously, as actual and spiritual, manifest and intentional. The intrinsic magic of this act is in the absolution of the past, the commitment to the present, and its reverberation into the future. With such concentration the immaterial can materialize as the fruit of experience.

Divinatory Meaning

Absolution, the purification of the self by selfless action. Dedication of all action to the higher source so that all such action can become one's *sadhana,* an act in which one is conscious of the spiritual nature of all the parts. Elevation of the mundane and temporal to the divine. To make a practice of self-disciplined action. Humility, adaptation, the development of the Will along a spiritual path. The fruit of such endeavor. At the Base it relates to worldly acts; in the Spleen center it suggests the need for discipline as regards diet and the assimilatory function; in the Navel it shows the psychological position of purification; in the Heart it suggests spiritual fulfillment; in the Throat or Head, the teacher.

15

Ally

ALLY bears the number "15," the combination of the number ten of completion with the number five of organization. It signifies the raw power of the unconscious, in a blatant or erotic sense, the material of all intentional magical acts. This card is related to the Devil of the traditional Tarot.

Standing on the shores of a lake of molten lava the figure of an

Ally is depicted breathing out fire from jaws filled with spike-like teeth, symbolizing his power to destroy and devour. In both hands he holds double hooks, revealing his dual function as a catcher of souls and their controller. His body and head have all the marks of the lower orders of beings; ears, horns, scales, etc., which form his armor. His head is adorned with six grotesque bestial heads, his epaulets are animal heads and his nether regions are composed of another demonic face. His function here is as a destroyer of enemies, for those can only be caught who have something to hide or fear.

Divinatory Meaning

The person who draws this card has been given this creature as an Ally to help overcome lower orders of consciousness. The Ally is a form of the basic raw kundalini fire, the serpent-energy of the sexual center, at the Base region of the Tree of Life. However this energy is here expressed in an untransformed state. The Ally card is to be understood as a psychic tool, to be used when situations of negative outside influence need to be overthrown. If regressive or destructive aspects of the self need to be caught or burnt up, the drawing of this card will indicate that help is on the way. One should never be afraid of the Ally, or else he will gain ascendancy. The Ally is one of the guardians of the inner mandala, the mystic body as a circle of protection, and should be meditated on as such and befriended. The location of this card in the Tree of Life reading indicates the nature of the Ally's influence. At the Base it indicates the raw unconscious; in the Heart, the need to overcome fear.

16

Holocaust

HOLOCAUST bears the number "16," signifying spiritual victory and related to the cosmic function of the sun. This card relates to the Tower of the traditional Tarot.

A house is depicted in a state of demolition by fire. Rubble is heaped on the ground as the material edifice of reality crumbles and burns. This is an unpredicted event, breaking down the ego-roles of everyday existence, as is here symbolized by the suburban nature of the edifice. As the transforming fire of the Base center takes control, along with the flames, there bursts forth a cascade of eyes, symbolizing the loss of ego and the shedding of preconceptions brought about by the sudden traumatic event. The loss is seen here as a revelation, for not a single ego but rather the collective unconscious is involved and transformed.

Divinatory Meaning

The necessity to change one's standpoint, to take decisive dramatic action. Such action is basically on the self, to rid it of all confusion caused by ego motivation, to free oneself from all worldly attachments and securities. Also this card suggests an event which reverberates on a wider level, a public catharsis, bringing about a general change of consciousness. A person receiving this card should therefore consider that all events in the outside world are but reflections of inner needs, desires and motivations, and that shock tactics can be consciously employed so that one becomes aware of being the cause of a situation as well as receiving the effect. In such a way one can mirror the times and transcend all events comprising this Kali Yuga, the dark age when materiality, lack of moral fiber and general apathy prevail. This card is understood according to the location in the Tree of Life. At the Heart center it indicates a sudden emotional change.

17

Island of Jewels

ISLAND OF JEWELS bears the number "17," signifying the inner light of spiritual attainment through an exalted path of occultism, as suggested by the numbers "1" and "7" combined together. This card relates to the Star of the traditional Tarot.

In a whirlpool of clouds high above the earth as viewed from outer space there floats an island composed of colored jewels, beyond which is an infinite night sky filled with galaxies of stars. The island is situated in a place conceived of as being outside of the influence of time and is the visualization of the ideal self, the adamantine body of light. The island consists of twelve jewels symbolizing the exalted zodiac signs around a central crystal of the self, which here is shown as comprised of all the celestial forces that influence the world, with their force-fields of attraction and repulsion. It is understood as being not bound to the world but above it, as a pure transmitter and receiver of the celestial influences.

Divinatory Meaning

This is a highly auspicious boon card, suggesting the realization of hopes and aspirations achieved through the opening of the inner eye of the spirit and the development of the faculties of visualization. The key is to maintain faith in the higher Self, the resting ground of the deepest aspirations of the heart and soul, seeking expressions for them in this world, thereby laying the foundations for realization and illumination in the next. This card suggests an optimistic outlook and indicates success wherever it may be located in the Tree of Life. The psychological stance of this card is one of inspiration and insight: a spiritual breakthrough. Meditate on the limitless possibilities of the spirit.

18

Soma

SOMA bears the number "18," signifying the entry of forces from the secret realms of the psyche and the assimilation of these forces as fulfillment. It is the number of higher initiation, suggesting the unfolding of occult powers and the path of spiritual evolution. This card relates to the Moon of the traditional Tarot.

A type of sacred mushroom is depicted as a cosmic house of

light, the container of the distilled essence of the personality, the Soma or cooling fulfillment-aspect of the psyche.

The image of the mushroom is depicted as a mirage or shadow, almost flickering against the side of a white glacier. Soma, the magic mushroom, provides the doorway to realms of hidden knowledge, extraterrestrial forces and spiritual enlightenment, but is not these things *in themselves*. It is only in the interaction of the Soma with the psyche, the inner water with the inner fire, that resolution of potencies can take place. Thus the mushroom is here depicted as being intangible, the glacier being like the tip of the iceberg beneath which are the unfathomable depths of the universal mind. The mushroom is also a simile for the moon, in her function as reflector of light and distiller of wisdom. Soma is the elixir, the taste of enlightenment, the lunar wisdom-drops, situated in the Head center of the subtle body and symbolized in the Tree of Life chart as a crescent moon pointing downward and exuding drops.

Divinatory Meaning

Intuition, imagination. This card relates to the Head center and suggests that wisdom is attainable through the distillation of all experience. It potentizes the dream world and the realm of visionary experience. It represents female intuitive wisdom (the moon) as the counterpart to the masculine fiery drive (the sun). It is the completion of the ascent through the psychic centers (chakras).

19

Phoenix

The PHOENIX card bears the number "19," signifying the ultimate mystical attainment, as is suggested by the combination of the number of unity "1" with the number of completion "9." This card relates to the Sun of the traditional Tarot.

From an alchemical fire of transformation, there rises up an eternal flame burning up the past and all illusion. From the flame a

Cosmic Couple is born in divine union, the Celestial Buddha Vajradhara and his consort, rising as a phoenix from the ashes of the temporal body. They are colored blue, symbolizing the complementary aspects of the celestial voidness as Wisdom and Means, and winged, indicating their transcendant spiritual nature. They are the produced Philosopher's Stone, described in the classical texts of the school of Agrippa as "fed with the fire of the Father and the ether of the Mother, the first of which may be understood allegorically as food and the second as drink, without which the phoenix will not attain full glory." The text continues, "feed thy bird and it will move in the nest and then rise up like a star of the firmament." On *The Tantric Dakini Oracle* card the red star ruby suggests this concept.

Divinatory Meaning

Rebirth, the rays of the sun re-emerging after the darkness of night. Liberation of the spirit previously imprisoned in matter. Fire levels all things, reducing all the structures of mankind to ashes. Out of the ashes of the fire of passion there rises the capacity for selfless love. Meditate on this aspect and on its powers of transmutation, for to love is to see love everywhere and in all things. The indication of this card is success, in the place located in the Tree of Life. At the Base center it may indicate marriage; in the Heart, an affair. In the Head, it tells of fulfillment.

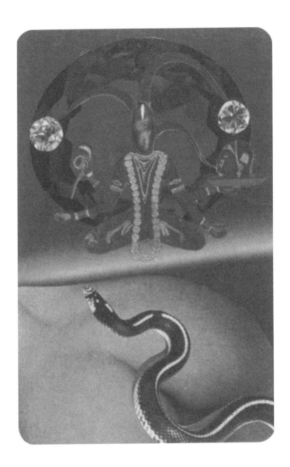

20

Transformation

TRANSFORMATION bears the number "20," signifying duality united and integrated as a position of tantric potency. This card relates to the Judgment of the Tarot.

The lower part of this card depicts the Base region of a female body, with a snake uncoiling and moving in an upward direction. This symbolizes the awakened serpent power, the kundalini-energy, commencing a journey through the subtle centers of the body. It shows the raw shakti as energy in its gross form. The upper part shows the same energy in a transformed and elevated state. The intersection of the two is marked by a rainbow band of light, indicating the threshold where experience becomes attainment.

On the rainbow there is seated a form of a tantric goddess, known as Chinnamasta. She is in lotus posture, with four hands and her body the color of the inner central psychic subtle channel. She represents the channeling of energy upward to the fulfillment stage where psychic balance is all-important. She holds a kundalini-serpent, which indicates that she has harnessed the raw energy of the Base center, a skull-bowl filled with blood (symbolizing her position of renunciation and compassion), an elixir-fruit suggesting the transformation into the realm of eternity, and a plate supporting her own decapitated head (symbolizing her egoless self-transcendence). From her neck flow three streams of blood, indicating that the three main psychic arteries are opened to receive fulfillment. Around her neck she wears a garland of skulls telling of her evocation of the subtle primordial matrix vibrations of which the whole universe is comprised. In the position of her head, at the neck, there is placed a fine sapphire, meaning that the original voidness of space is inherent in her. This card is the visual representation of the process of alchemy in balance and reflected in the transformation body of fulfillment. This image is the expression of tantric mystery.

Divinatory Meaning

A highly auspicious card, indicating a fine level of self-development achieved. It suggests spiritual awakening, renewal, ecstasy achieved through balanced union, fulfillment. In the world location (at the Base center) it suggests judgment in one's favor. The supremacy of the higher over the lower, spirit over matter.

21

Earthbound

EARTHBOUND bears the number "21," signifying development from the world upward, through the subtle centers to the stage of fulfillment in life. This card relates to the World of the traditional Tarot.

The surface of the earth viewed from space lies below. Above the horizon the orb of a new earth is seen as if suspended in the darkness of the night. This symbolizes the beginning inherent in every completed cycle. As we step out of one situation, beyond our roots (suggested by the surface of the earth), the next moment manifests itself in the completeness of the new perspective. By our nature we are destined to return to the earth until the completion of the cycles of incarnation.

Divinatory Meaning

Realization of the underlying meaning of earthly existence. The completion of a cycle. Responsibility, understood in its broader aspect as humanitarianism. Action as the result of choice and free will. Liberation from the bondage of a habit. Change in viewpoint. Could indicate a change in residence. Parallel universes and the concept of new things emerging from the old. This card relates to karma and should be meditated upon with this in mind. Single-mindedness, particularly with regard to worldly things. The location of this card in the Tree of Life chart indicates the nature of the interpretation. At the Base center it tells of a worldly psychological position; in the Spleen, of a possible health hazard. At the Heart it is an emotional obstacle which keeps the questions fixed to worldliness. In the Throat and Head locations it relates to psychological goals, telling of a potential change in viewpoint.

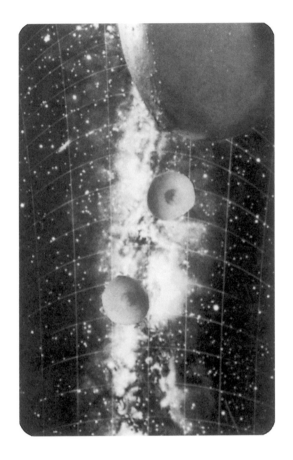

22

Mother's Milk

MOTHER'S MILK bears the number "22," signifying the combined essential mother-principles of attachment and nourishment. According to the classification by elements this is an Air card, normally related to the suit of Swords in the traditional Tarot Minor Arcana.

On an astronomical map of the Milky Way two small breasts

appear to be floating in space. At the top right hand corner is depicted a voluptuous breast, suggesting the maternal principle, whose breast-milk has here become the Milky Way. This card evokes the desire to reach back to the original Mother, the great nourisher of this universe. The two smaller breasts represent the original unity manifesting as *prakriti*, the Nature principle, which materializes as all worlds and all phenomena. This is the mystery of great Nature.

Divinatory Meaning

Spiritual homesickness, the desire to get back to the primal source, just as a baby longs to suckle the breast of the mother. It represents the aspiration for non-duality and can indicate that the questioner should recognize the need for nourishment. According to the placement of this card on the Tree of Life chart the emphasis and meaning is made clear. At the Base center it means with regard to the world, at the Spleen center it relates to nourishment as health, in the Heart center it is concerned with emotion such as with regard to a lover or child. At the Throat center the indication is toward the need for fulfillment in the realm of fantasy and the imagination. At the Head center the card tells of spiritual nourishment as the outcome from a higher Self. Honoring the female principle of fecundity and generation, meditate on the bounteous nature of the infinite. Remember that each one of us has been nourished by great Nature.

23

Maya: How She Spins

MAYA: HOW SHE SPINS bears the number "23," signifying the combination of complementary opposites united with the threefold truth of all existence (as for Creation, Preservation, and Dissolution). This number also suggests a midway point through which all sensory experiences converge, as a hub of a wheel which emanates everything. According to the classification by elements this is an Air card, normally related to the suit of Swords in the Minor Arcana of the traditional Tarot.

High amongst swirling cloud forms over the earth viewed from space sits an old woman, a form of Mahamaya, the Great Illusion, working on her spinning wheel. She is spinning the original yarn which will make up the fabric of all existence. Her position, high in space, suggests her detachment from the things of the world. As the Great Illusion, she is capable of taking any form. Her personification as an old woman or fairy tale witch warns us not to be seduced by the beauteous forms which she sometimes inhabits, thereby catching us in the web of delusion, making us mere puppets of her play. The wheel on which she spins represents the great Wheel of Time, on which the cycles of existence are formed and out of which all karmas emerge.

Divinatory Meaning

Recognize that youth, beauty, old-age, ugliness and death are but transient phenomena, the production of Mother Maya, the Great Illusion. See through the fabric of existence and try to understand the cause behind each worldly situation. This card indicates the need to withdraw from the ways of the world and to locate oneself in the position of the spinner. This is the way that personal destiny can be transformed. The position in the Tree of Life chart indicates the field of reference. At the Base region the card relates to a passing out of a cycle of destiny and a possible sexual entanglement. In the Spleen it refers to assimilation; in the Heart, to psychological attitudes. In the Throat and Head the card tells of the possibility of controlling destiny.

24

Solar Return

SOLAR RETURN bears the number "24," signifying the cycles of time resolved and returned to a cosmic point of reference, the integration of opposites in balance, the number of stability in the microcosmic-macrocosmic relationship. According to the classification by elements this is an Air card, normally related to the suit of Swords in the Minor Arcana of the traditional Tarot.

The image consists of a solar eclipse forming a black sun with a corona of light seemingly contracting and receding into the center. This symbolizes the archetypal forces of heaven, influencing through the stars, planets and lunar cycles, forming subtle tides of destiny. The eternal recurrence, as light recedes into darkness through the completion of an aeon of time. The card evokes the concept of a black sun or black hole, from which a new reality emerges. This is the abstract image of Great Time, another aspect of Mahakali, the devouring and creating principle of all experience.

Divinatory Meaning

Return to the roots of the personality. Consider the astrological influences at birth, in order to find the path of least resistance in the present situation. Try to decipher the past in order to predict the future. Bring the future into the present. This card relates to the "Darkening of the Light" hexagram of the I-Ching, but presents a time when one may be forced to confront the inner structure of the psyche. The relationship of the individual to the collective unconcious is to be considered. The overcoming of obstacles through recognition of self-nature; the calculation of exterior influences to compute one's evolutionary direction. Cultivate the faculty of being aware of auspicious signs such as dreams or omens. A positive card, very much the path of the warrior, a chance to make gains by confrontation, the burning of karma, a return to the source. A way through to eternity.

25

Threefold Riddle

THREEFOLD RIDDLE bears the number "25," signifying the cycle of psychological temptation and its resolution as direction, the highest attribute of which is the wisdom of discrimination. According to the classification by elements this is an Air card, normally related to the suit of Swords in the Minor Arcana of the traditional Tarot.

Out beyond the realms of the knowable, in the infinity of space, stand three veiled and mysterious figures. The veils are of the kind traditionally worn by Muslim women in Afghanistan, but they represent the unrevealed aspect of a triad of forces, the threefold nature of existence in the world. The figures are of like gender, either female or possibly asexual; their identity is concealed. The riddle is the secret nature of the questioner. The veils represent the clothing that the spirit takes on in order to manifest in the world, both as a protection and as an illusion. In this context they can be understood as guardians to the realm of Mahamaya, the Great Illusion. As such they urge mankind to try to understand the riddle of existence and at the same time confuse the seeker with their mysterious dance of illusion. This is a riddle card, a seduction through the mystery of a self which is concealed.

Divinatory Meaning

This card, more than any other in the deck, will have a meaning totally personal to the one who receives it. This is the riddle card, yet the riddle is knowable through that part of the self which has remained concealed. Therefore the interpretation of this card is very personal, according to its location on the Tree of Life chart. It is best understood by meditating on the riddle card in its place on the chat, all the while remembering the question originally addressed to the oracle. Look into the depths of the unconscious mind. A location of this card at the Base center suggests vestiges of past karma still influencing the present; in the Spleen center, a possible health problem due to imbalance of assimilation factors; in the Navel center, a riddle with respect to the question or the psychological stance of the questioner. At the Heart location it points to the need to open up the emotions; in the Throat, a riddle in the dream realm. In the Head, the Oracle should be reconsulted.

26

Mean and Heavy

MEAN AND HEAVY bears the number "26," signifying the position of evolutionary responsibility through the communication between the unconscious and conscious parts of the universal mind. According to the classification by elements this is an Air card, normally related to the suit of Swords in the Minor Arcana of the traditional Tarot.

Striding through the cosmos comes the goddess Kali, in the guise of an avenging angel. Her black boots indicate that her mission is earth-bound, her bodiless head tells that it requires the single-minded execution of right action. She is in a wrathful aspect, black as limitless space, symbolizing that the essence of wrath is voidness. Manifested from the serene mind-sky of Buddha-essence, she comes into the world as the protector of the *dharma* (the cosmic truth), ruthlessly consuming the poisons of the three times (the past, present, and future), symbolized by the three skulls trampled under foot and by the three skull ornaments. Her long red tongue is extended, indicating that her essence is projected into the world to consume all poisons. In her black hand she holds by the hair the four heads of the demons of greed, jealousy, morbidity and deceit. Her eyes are wide open as an invitation into her all-seeing nature. She is the form of Kali, brought into being to conquer the demons of decadent materialism in the Kali Yuga, the present age. Though wrathful in appearance, she is filled with compassion.

Divinatory Meaning

Do not be fearful in taking a strong line in the present situation. Be prepared to fight any enemy of the truth (in oneself and in others), for such action is the sign of the times. Recognize the nature of the present age and take right action. Do not become mean and heavy as the world is, but rather mean and heavy with the direct discriminating wisdom of right action. At the Base center this card relates to the worldly stance and also to the sexual area; in the Spleen, to assimilation factors such as food and habits; in the Navel, to one's psychological position. At the Heart center the indication is of detachment from the emotional body (where feelings rule the mind) in order to act by one's higher convictions. This card always suggests great potency for resolution, for cutting through, and should be so acted upon.

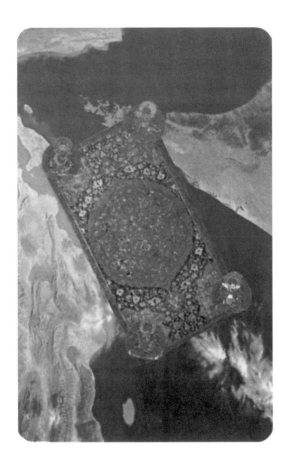

27

Magic Carpet

MAGIC CARPET bears the number "27," signifying the positive influence of occult or celestial forces from above. It is the mystic number of the asterisms, the star-groups influencing the psyche, or a higher harmonic of the astral light. According to the classification by elements this is an Air card normally related to the suit of Swords in the Minor Arcana of the traditional Tarot.

As if viewed from outer space, an exotic oriental carpet is seen flying high above the Persian Gulf. The image is a representation of the powers of transport and elevation inherent in the mind, for a magic carpet is a flight of fancy. Four Celestial Buddhas sit at each corner of the carpet, in male/female aspect in tantric embrace. They are like guardians of the four directions of the inner mandala, the mystic circle of psychic protection. These Buddhas represent the ecstasy of transport out of the physical body and indicate the formalization or crystallization of the powers of visualization.

Divinatory Meaning

Transport, in the literal (if located in the worldly parts of the Tree of Life chart) or spiritual sense. Can indicate a change of residence, especially if in the Base center; otherwise, a development of the faculties of imagination, of visualization, particularly if located in the Throat or Head centers. A strong desire not to be bound up by the physical world and its habitual patterns. As an influence on the Heart center it suggests the entering in of a new way of reacting, possibly with regard to spiritual instructions or a spiritual teacher coming into one's field of reference. This is a very favorable card, auspiciousness manifested potently, the uplifting of every situation. Meditate on this card as a form of the liberated spirit, the astral body, higher aspirations along ecstatic lines and the potency of a moment of harmony and balance. It evokes the concept of a vehicle linking the worlds of reality and surreality.

28

Cosmic Carrot

COSMIC CARROT bears the number "28," signifying the high potency of the occult transmission. This is the perfect multiple of the number seven, an expression of the mystic teachings, related to the inner protective circle of the self. According to the classification by elements this is an Air card, normally related to the suit of Swords in the Minor Arcana of the traditional Tarot.

Up in the clouds a carrot of unlimited dimension is dangled. This is the bait from the realms of higher consciousness, the home of the gods. The trunk of the carrot is marked by the six different psychic centers, or chakras, of the subtle body. These centers represent the awakening of the latent potential within the gross body, and the opening up of its subtle pathways to the celestial influences of many different orders of magnitude. When the psychic centers are opened, the gods, or higher psychological attitudes, come and rest within these centers. From the Base upward they are, respectively, Ganesha the Elephant-headed Lord of Obstacles, Brahma the Lord of Creation, Vishnu the Lord of Preservation, and Maheshwara the Lord of Dissolution. At the topmost center, in the Head region, sit the Divine Lovers, Shiva and Parvati, in the ecstasy of their union. The development of the subtle body is the doorway to the liberation of the self, and in this respect the Cosmic Carrot represents the thought of enlightenment.

Divinatory Meaning

An earnest desire of the questioner for liberation and enlightenment. This card suggests that enlightened states of existence are to be gained through the transformation of the self, by ingesting the spiritual teachings offered and by working on the self so that it becomes a fit vehicle for such consciousness. This card may indicate the need for spiritual/physical discipline, such as yoga or meditation. In the upper locations it suggests that such a path has been taken and will come to fruition. It is a very occult-oriented card.

29

Self-Preservation

SELF-PRESERVATION bears the number "29," signifying initiation into the timeless wisdom-aspect of exalted femininity. According to the classification by elements this is an Air card, normally related to the suit of Swords in the Minor Arcana of the traditional Tarot.

On the brink of eternity, swept over by the winds of change, stands a beautifully decorated Egyptian mummy as a symbol of the immortal body of eternity. The serenity of the face indicates the passive attitude of the higher spirit to the passing of all the things of the world. The two arms are shown crossed over at the breast, suggesting the concept of eternal preservation through the balance of all the forces of time. The mystic immortal spirit, or *ka*, is shown as a bird with wings outstretched, just below the two crossed hands. This card expresses the concept of a self worthy of preservation, as the spirit which will outlast all worldly change.

Divinatory Meaning

A wish to maintain self-integrity through all types of changing phenomena. If the questioner of the oracle finds that his position in the world or with regard to a personal relationship is being threatened, then the drawing of this card indicates the need to withdraw into oneself the life-force (the *prana-vayu*) in order to maintain equilibrium. Recognize the need for self-preservation in the area which this card falls within. If located in the Base center, the suggestion is of past influences related to a difficult childhood, even of illness, so heightening the sense of survival in the self. In the Spleen center, the indication is the need to take care of health. At the Navel center there is every reason to see the concept of self-preservation as the psychological stance adopted by the questioner. At the Heart center the emotional attitude is indicated; in the Throat center, the recognition of the primacy of the creative aesthetic. Meditate on the egoless self, maintaining the inner flame or truth, beyond all dualities.

30

Castles in the Clouds

CASTLES IN THE CLOUDS bears the number "30," signifying the higher development of the Will. According to the classification by elements this is an Air card, normally related to the suit of Swords in the Minor Arcana of the traditional Tarot.

High up, in the clouds of the mind-sky a turreted fairytale castle of stone is seen floating. The clouds represent the screen on which the vision of self is projected, the castle itself being the manifestation of the hopes and aspirations of the questioner. It is the home of the sky-walkers, those aspects of personality which derive energy from the power of fantasy. This card represents an alternative reality to the mundane world, for the stones of the castle are made out of a subtle mind-stuff, the material of the imagination.

Divinatory Meaning

Follow through your deepest wishes with the power of the Will. Do not allow any bodily laziness to prevent inner desires from becoming realities. This card suggests a vivid imagination, particularly when it falls in the Throat center of the Tree of Life chart, but coupled with a lack of creative fulfillment or a difficulty in communication with others. At the Base center there is an indication of past influences of the questioner being in the realm of mind-dreams, at the Spleen center the suggestion is that the health will benefit from a more earth-related diet, with the power of the Will discriminating a balanced food intake. At the Navel the psychological position of the questioner is indicated, and at the Heart or Head centers there is an indication that a change of residence may be the outcome to the question. Meditate on the unity of projection and introjection, the Will and the Wish. Recognize the positive power of the imagination but at the same time realize that without the ability to act decisively there will be no completion or fulfillment. Try to put one's direction toward the completion of work already commenced.

31

Just Passing Through

JUST PASSING THROUGH bears the number "31," signifying the recognition of the principles of trinity and unity combined together as the expression of the fundamental truth of worldly existence. According to the classification by elements this is the last, or tenth, of the Air cards, normally related to the suit of Swords in the Minor Arcana of the traditional Tarot.

A single huge wing of the bird of the psyche is shown entering and about to leave the field of vision; there are clouds stretching out into the sky behind and several rivers of the earth visible below. There is no indication that the single wing has any head or other parts, confirming that this symbol does not refer to a particular aspect of personality but rather to the air-freed spirit liberated from any kind of temporal situation. This is the sign of the spirit not trapped within any particular limits of form but instead capable of assuming any requirement through the attitude of the Will. It signifies the acceptance of the truth of existence in the world as being but a series of events through which one must pass without becoming entrapped.

Divinatory Meaning

The questioner feels as if a visitor to the situation under consideration. This position is one which has no fixed responsibility, and which may be either positive or negative depending on the nature of the other cards in the reading and on the placement of this card in the Tree of Life chart. In the Heart center it shows the tendency to transcend the heaviness of emotional ties to the world, an acceptance of the free nature of the spirit. In the Throat center the indication is of new ideas from the environment, and in the Head center it can represent the natural inclination toward higher consciousness as the outcome. Meditate on this card as the bird of the self.

32

Shiva: The Pillar of Fire

SHIVA: THE PILLAR OF FIRE bears the number "32," signifying the Astral Light coming from the fulfillment of spiritual ideals. This numerological concept is related to the psychic center (chakra) of the Head region, which has traditionally thirty-two downward emanating rays, and to the final thirty-second Path of Malkuth in the Kabbalistic system. According to the classification by elements this is the first of the Fire cards, normally related to the suit of Wands in the Minor Arcana of the traditional Tarot.

From behind the crest of a falling wave, conceived of as washing through all dualities, there rises an enormous pillar of fire. The central flame is wrapped in fire from the surface of the sun, the divine fire of Lord Shiva, a pillar with neither top nor bottom. This image represents the unity of Brahma the Creator (as the fire of the sun), Vishnu the Preserver (as the cosmic waters) and Maheshwara Shiva the Dissolver (as the Pillar of Fire, the Consumer) the whole glyph indicating the power of fulfillment through the inexhaustible self-created shiva lingam, the phallus of enlightenment. In alchemy it is the refining fire, bringing about the transmutation of all elements.

Divinatory Meaning

This card represents a moment of illumination, a revelation, an understanding of the miraculous nature of all things in their essence. It is the vision of the end of the world, the consuming Pillar of Fire, a cosmic phallus without beginning or end, the impregnator of the world to come. It indicates a positive turning point in the life of the questioner, a highly charged moment, defined by the place of this card in the Tree of Life chart. At the Base center it shows a potent sexual charge, awakening and sending the kundalini-energy upward, so illuminating the subtle body. At the Spleen center the indication is of a healthy digestion assisting the questioner. In the Navel center it shows a potent psychological breakthrough and in the Heart region, a great personal force, both attractive and transforming.

33

Eternal Life

ETERNAL LIFE bears the number "33," signifying the mystic completion of the threefold cycle of existence (as Creation, Preservation and Dissolution), the eternal resting-place of the exalted psyche. According to the classification by elements this a Fire card, normally related to the suit of Wands in the Minor Arcana of the traditional Tarot.

The Egyptian god Amen stands before the primordial waters which have turned to gold by the light of the sun's orb shining above. The eternal figure of Amen holds the Ankh, the mystic looped cross, the symbol of eternal life, as if to catch or reflect the rays of the sun. Below, to the right is the great sphinx, here indicating that the solution to her riddle is to be found in the path leading to eternal life. The sphinx is the symbol of the alchemical agent or catalyst, whose inner nature holds the key to the process of transformation, producing the substance which can turn all matter to gold, all spirits to the enlightened. The raw material is the person, the distilled elixir is the immortal spirit of eternity.

Divinatory Meaning

The solution of a problem, the triumph of light over darkness, clarity over obscurity, just as the sun rises each morning after the night is completed. This card indicates interest in other forms of existence, in the concept of reincarnation and an acceptance deep within the psyche of the cycles of rebirth. A need to create that which will outlast the single life span. It suggests an elevation of whichever center in which it falls. It is a highly fortunate card, indicating the resolution of the question or the fulfillment of a particular task or cycle of activity. At the Base center there is an indication of the practical application of alchemical concepts. At the Spleen center it particularly suggests strength of health; in the Navel center, the conservation of energy. At the Heart region the card tells of the emotions transcended or even exalted to become higher ideals, depending on the influences. In the Head center the card tells of fulfillment, in both a worldly and a spiritual context, according to the question put to the oracle.

34

Burning Bush / Lineage Tree

BURNING BUSH/LINEAGE TREE bears the number "34," signifying the completion of occult preparation. According to the classification by elements this is a Fire card, normally related to the suit of Wands in the Minor Arcana of the traditional Tarot.

In the center of a reddish-leaved tree, symbolizing the passionate fiery nature of tantric revelation, the hierarch Karmapa sits on a lotus, the sign of his spiritual exaltation. He is the embodiment of the tantric transmission, the occult teachings of Tibet. As the expression of celestial compassion, he is crowned with the mystic *vajra mukut* (the black hat) of the dakinis. It is said that the mere sight of this crown is sufficient to evoke the urge for enlightenment. In one hand the lama holds the *mahamudra* book of tantric practices, which teach the shortest way to enlightenment within a lifetime. The other hand bestows blessings with an outstretched mystic gesture. The flames tell of the inner spiritual fire of conviction and a halo, suggesting that spirituality is all-encompassing. Above the head a rainbow spectrum of light beams indicates the hot line to the spiritual lineage. This lama-figure represents true compassionate wisdom, self-incarnated through the yoga of consciousness-transmission. The whole tree is itself supported by a most beautiful lotus, pointing to the spirituality inherent within.

Divinatory Meaning

A highly favorable and auspicious card, indicating an opportunity or need for the questioner to connect directly with a lineage of mystic teachings. The card presents a moment of insight and revelation. At any place on the Tree of Life chart it should be meditated upon as a place of refuge. This card also suggests that deeper feelings of faith are being evoked or tested. It tells of the need of the questioner to eliminate all doubts about the future. Do not hesitate, be firm in your convictions about the task ahead. Honor the existence of metaphysical authorities and do not doubt their compassionate nature.

35

As Above/So Below

AS ABOVE/SO BELOW bears the number "35," signifying resolution of complementary cycles of activity. According to the classification by elements this is a Fire card, normally related to the suit of
Wands in the Minor Arcana of the traditional Tarot.

A flowery mandala is depicted set against a background of mysterious mountains glowing in the morning light of a new day. In the

world below, the raw energy of the earth is seen bursting forth as molten lava from a volcano. Above is the refined essence of consciousness, suggested by the quality of the light and the expectancy of the fresh air and space. The flower is as if projected on the mind-sky from the clouds or mountains, mirroring itself to produce the rich image of purple and red in the form of a mandala or mystic protective enclosure. In the two worlds of above and below it mirrors itself to form a single unity. As has been attributed to the Emerald Tablet of Hermes the supreme alchemist: "That which is above is as that which is below, and that which is below is as that which is above, for performing the miracles of the One Thing. Thou shalt separate the earth from the fire, the subtle from the gross, gently and with much care. It ascends from earth to heaven and again descends to earth, so receiving the strength of both superior and inferior things. By this means you will have the glory of the world, and because of it all obscurity will leave you."

Divinatory Meaning

This is very much a Heart card, indicating an opening of the Heart center and the subsequent refinement of the emotions. A very favorable card, whatever the position of the Tree of Life chart, reminding the questioner of the truth beyond all dualities. At the lower centers the indication is of a need to relate worldly situations to an overall metaphysical viewpoint. It tells of the inexhaustible power of the Heart. In the Head or Heart centers this card suggests attainment of balance and insight into the mysteries of metaphysics.

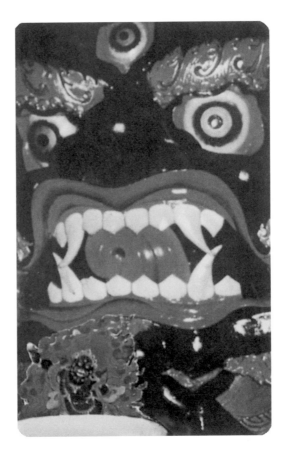

36

Guardian

GUARDIAN bears the number "36," signifying entry into the higher tantric initiations. According to the classification by elements this is a Fire card, normally related to the suit of Wands in the Minor Arcana of the traditional Tarot.

The huge terrifying face of Mahakala, the great tantric guardian and occult personification of Great Time, fills the card. He is depicted holding a skull-bowl from which a smaller form of himself surrounded by flames is seen to emerge. As a wrathful deity he is depicted with an open fanged mouth, wide bloodshot eyes, and fiery eyebrows. The skull-bowl is the symbol of renunciation from the ways of the world and the recognition of the power inherent in the tantric path. This aspect is the guardian of the Kargyudpa lineage (the tantric sect) of Tibet, whose mystic form is conceived of as resting within the cavern of the Heart. On the Tree of Life chart, a form of Mahakala is depicted at the Heart center. The third eye of the Guardian denotes the penetration and all-seeing nature of this concept. The curled tongue is a sign of the spiral or cyclical nature of all existence.

Divinatory Meaning

This card represents the presence of a most potent form of protection. Mahakala is the devourer of all the enemies of truth, burning up all illusion, and both swallowing and creating karmas the patterns of destiny. The drawing of this card indicates the presence of a guardian angel at the area of the subtle body where located. In the Base center it suggests firm roots, at the Spleen center there is a danger of a possible digestive malfunction or an energy leak on the psychic level of entities or spirits. At the Navel center it denotes a guiding presence; at the Heart the suggestion is of high potency and fulfillment. At the Throat it is psychic protection; and in the Head, the potential of contact with an occult lineage.

37

Fire of Sacrifice

FIRE OF SACRIFICE bears the number "37," signifying the occult path of commitment. According to the classification by elements this is a Fire card, normally related to the suit of Wands in the Minor Arcana of the traditional Tarot.

The card depicts great tongues of flame consuming all things. The charred surface of the earth is like a playground for volcanic eruption, as the fires of the interior break loose. The fire in the foreground represents the personal fire of renunciation, the inner flame of concentration and conviction. This is set against a background suggesting the temporal nature of all things. The fire as evoked by this card symbolizes the disciplining of body, speech and mind as a metaphysical sacrifice and offering.

Divinatory Meaning

Recognize the ability of the self to let go of all habits and habit-forming thoughts. Replace these with conscious rituals of worship. A deliberate act of self sacrifice may be necessary to the questioner who draws this card. If this is consciously practiced a great advantage is to be gained. Let go of all worldly attachments (possessiveness) in favor of the inner fire of faith, keeping this constant in the illusory field of existence. If this card is located in the Base center the indication is of the burning up of past karma with respect to the world, a break with the past and a possible sexual awakening in the future. In the Spleen center the suggestion is of an aid to the digestive and assimilative function. At the Navel the psychological position of the questioner is presented, indicating that it is the fire of faith which allows the secrets of the dakinis to become known. In the Heart center a passionate consuming affair is indicated; at the Throat, psychic penetration; and in the Head, an act of selfless sacrifice leading to the transformation of a situation.

38

A-Musement

A-MUSEMENT bears the number "38," signifying the female power-principle (shakti) channeled along an occult path of fulfillment. According to the classification by elements this is a Fire card, normally related to the suit of Wands in the Minor Arcana of the traditional Tarot.

In a red-hot center of volcanic fire, symbolizing awakened and expressed passion and attraction, the force of the active female shakti-principle is represented by a white dakini (an embodiment of female wisdom-energy) pictured as a sensuous alluring woman accompanied by six attendants. They are all adorned with the symbolic ornaments of initiation, revealing that tantric union within the occult circle is known as the initiation into the mandala of the self. Here the female power-principle is shown awakened within woman, who is worshipped as the goddess of all creation. The consummation of the union is symbolized by the flower of bliss rising from the sexual area of the woman. Wine is offered as part of the left-hand tantric ritual, suggesting that the spiritual path may be likened to intoxication with the divine. The whole card represents the appreciation and enjoyment of the female principle; a potent mystical experience leading to fulfillment. The goddess as the muse of tantra.

Divinatory Meaning

The promise of pleasure and fulfillment. The real integration of sensual and spiritual aspects of nature. When this card is located at the Base center the suggestion is of the questioner moving upward through the ground of sexuality. At the Spleen center it indicates letting go of rigid ideas concerning lifestyle, while at the Navel center the psychological indication is of transformation through the tantric rituals of the conscious blending of the senses. At the Heart the card tells of a deep love and respect for the mystic aspects of the female principle, with the indication of a fruitful and fulfilling love affair. At the Throat the realm of sexual fantasy is invoked by this card, particularly in the environment. In the Head location the indication is of a mystic initiation through spontaneity.

39

Serpent Power

SERPENT POWER bears the number "39," signifying the power at the root of mystical transformation. According to the classification by elements this is a Fire card, normally related to the suit of Wands in the Minor Arcana of the traditional Tarot.

From the base of the card a large hooded cobra uncoils, stretching its head upward toward the sky. This is the symbol of the awakening kundalini, the serpent-energy latent within each psyche, centered at the Base region of the subtle body. Behind the snake a huge flash of lightning illuminates the sky, suggesting the tremendous charge of energy accompanying the release of the raw power of the psyche. The card as a whole represents the cosmic potential of the kundalini energy, and its tendency to move upward, breaking through all barriers.

Divinatory Meaning

An awakening of latent powers. A sudden burst of high energy and the ability to use it to manifest evolutionary changes in the realm of the world. Bear in mind the importance of the proper use of such energy. If this card falls in the Base center of the Tree of Life chart it indicates a sexual awakening with a potent possibility of channeling and utilizing this energy for both physical and psychological fulfillment. At the Spleen center the card tells of a fiery assimilative function, perhaps in need of careful control. When placed at the Navel center it indicates the potent power to transform all things with the single-minded application of the positive Will. In the Heart center the card suggests the desire for power in the world or in an emotional relationship, depending on the four influence cards. When at the Throat center there is a strong indication of sudden creative insight, possibly of a sexual or sexually symbolic origin, the power of the vision, the sublimated sexuality taking on form in the world for the transmission of visionary insight. Located in the Head center the card tells of the need to temper the visionary nature with the cooling drops of discriminating wisdom.

40

Blow Your Mind

BLOW YOUR MIND bears the number "40," signifying the completion of a period of intense self-discipline and the arrival at a sudden spiritual release. According to the classification by elements this is a Fire card, normally related to the suit of Wands in the Minor Arcana of the traditional Tarot.

From the stem of a water-pipe a smoking-bowl emerges, out of which an atom bomb explodes in a fiery mushroom. Several layers of red colored cloud-lights are formed and penetrated by the power of the explosion, appearing as a series of ascending veils. At the uppermost level a human brain is projected, symbolizing a dramatic change of consciousness. Just as the explosion of the atom bomb can change the whole mundane nature of existence, so the splitting of the atom of the psyche can change one's whole field of reference. This card shows the atomic nature of mind-stuff in its essence, pointing to the need to break through limits of worldly conditioning in order to achieve transcendence.

Divinatory Meaning

The time has come to change a point of view. Open up new channels in the mind, and do not allow yourself to become entrenched in old and habitual patterns of thought. The card suggests that the doorway through to the collective unconscious is perhaps to be entered through the storming of the barricades, by acting spontaneously and without reference to predictable patterns of behavior. Do not be restricted by your own petty limitations. When this card is located at the Base center it suggests the feeling of detachment from the world and entry into the dimension of spontaneity. At the Spleen center the indication is of a possible traumatic experience influencing the position of the self. The Navel center location gives the power of transformatory action with a potential for release; at the Heart region it tells of the strong desire of the questioner to be removed from an emotional entanglement or a carefree attitude, depending on the nature of the other four influences. When located in the Head it predicts a sudden spiritual release, a transcendant experience, attainable by an acceptance of the need to change one's restrictive attitude to life.

41

High Tension

HIGH TENSION bears the number "41," signifying the combination of great physical powers exerted through the Will. According to the classification by elements this is the last, or tenth, of the Fire cards, normally related to the suit of Wands in the Minor Arcana of the traditional Tarot.

Like a giant standing on the mountain peaks, the muscular body of a weight-lifter is depicted emitting flashes of lightning from the region of the throat. The body is without any head and the two hands rest on the hips of the figure. This card shows the human body as an energy-field, a conductor of currents, emitting positively charged energies in sudden flashes, yet pushed to the extremes, as is suggested by the expanded muscles and the gigantic proportions. The figure is like a landmark, a lighthouse, flashing waves of energy across the landscape below.

Divinatory Meaning

The questioner finds the need to take a firm position, as a warrior. This is an extremely uncomfortable situation to find oneself obliged to maintain, because of the constant outpouring of vast amounts of energy. Thus it is also a state of high tension, requiring the ability to relax and recuperate at the first possible opportunity. When this card is located at the Base center it indicates problems related to survival in the world, with the tendency for the self to become too programmed. There is also the indication of the life-force being awakened and channeled through the sexual area, but needing bodily relaxation in order to bring about psychological transmutation. At the Spleen center there is the sign of some digestive malfunction due to tension, such as from overwork, whereas at the Navel this card has the positive indication of a raw energy position ready for refinement. In the Heart center it tells of feelings at variance with the real position of the self; in the Throat there is a potency of sudden outbursts of creative Will, but also with a danger to health; and in the Head there is a need to change the lifestyle to one that will not produce high tension in the mind.

42

Wave of Bliss

WAVE OF BLISS bears the number "42," signifying harmony as an attribute of wisdom. According to the classification by elements, this is the first of the Water cards, normally related to the suit of Cups in the Minor Arcana of the traditional Tarot.

A huge wave, depicted at the moment of turning and breaking, sweeps across the foreground and appears as if mirrored in the background. This represents a moment quite outside of the realms of time; the ecstatic experience captured at its peak and contained within the ocean of the heart. The prow of a small boat, shown in the trough of the wave, indicates that the great tidal wave of ecstatic emotion is the leveler of all worldly projections, carrying with it everything that surrenders to its all-encompassing natural force. This card represents the dissolution of all dualities, reuniting all the parts of the psyche in the complete moment of cosmic orgasm.

Divinatory Meaning

A highly fortunate card, indicating the resolution of a problem and the washing away of any remaining attachment to personal limitations. It indicates consummation, of an erotic or spiritual nature, and the fruit of any physical or spiritual moment of union. It is a highly mystical card, suggesting that harmony can be achieved by plunging with faith into a situation, surrendering to the higher order of the Bliss Wave. When located at the Base center it points to the sexual fulfillment, the cooling waters of ecstasy; in the Navel, to the rebirth of personality through the shedding of ego-centered thinking. At the Heart center the indication is of an intense experience of higher love, either in a human relationship or in a purely mystical sense as spiritual completion. At the Throat region, mystical fulfillment leading to the highest delights. This card evokes the ecstatic potential inherent within.

43

Mount Meru: Center of the Universe

MOUNT MERU: CENTER OF THE UNIVERSE bears the number "43," signifying the integration of the inner and outer worlds, the microcosm with the macrocosm. According to the classification by elements this is a Water card, normally related to the suit of Cups in the Minor Arcana of the traditional Tarot.

In the midst of clouds on the roof of the world, the snowclad peak of a mountain appears. This represents the holy mountain, Mount Meru, which can be glimpsed only through the gap in the world of phenomenal appearance. According to Hindu tradition Mount Meru marks the mystic center of the Universe and is the abode of the Gods. Lord Shiva and his wife Parvati live there in their form of the Divine Couple. The holy mountain represents a place of great power, the centering process within the individual and the pivot of all exterior phenomena. It is represented in many different ways; like an enormous crystal, with sides of gold and precious jewels (as in the Map of the Universe chart), or as a great mountain pyramid, a place of pilgrimage. The actual Mount Meru is geographically located in Western Tibet and is known as Mount Kailash, a pilgrimage place for both Buddhists and Hindus.

Divinatory Meaning

A desire to forsake worldly ambition for the spiritual path. Disillusionment with worldly values and compromises, a reevaluation of one's position, possibly leading to the desire to withdraw from society. Mount Meru also is the symbol of rewards coming from work on oneself. Located at the Base position in the Tree of Life chart it suggests impending physical travel. At the Navel it denotes a strongly centered sense of identity, coupled with a firm Will and the ability to adapt without loss of integrity. In the Heart the indication is of emotional completion and at the Head location it represents uplifted consciousness and spiritual resolution, or the achievement of goals.

44

Heart Drop

HEART DROP bears the number "44," signifying initiation into a mystic or higher aspect of the self. According to the classification by elements this is a Water card, normally related to the suit of Cups in the Minor Arcana of the traditional Tarot.

In a limitless desert of white sand stands a stupa (a relic mound, containing the tantric teachings), emerging from a turquoise colored lake on whose shores many beautiful pink flowers grow. The whole scene is like a mirage of an oasis, representing the projection of the spiritual wish onto the vast pure land of unmanifest mind. From the third eye of the stupa three rubies fall, becoming a single heart-shaped ruby representing the distillation and crystallization of mystic experience. This is a mystic vision of the Heart Drop tantric teachings: the alchemical concept of integrating the male and female essence-principles, conceived as white and red distillations of wisdom and compassion, here symbolized by the pink flowers alongside the lake.

Divinatory Meaning

The distillation of experience and the joy of realization. This card represents the power of the heart as the seat of wisdom. Located in the Heart place on the Tree of Life chart, its natural home, it indicates the coming together of influences in the emotional realm, uplifted as a mystic initiation of deep significance to the questioner. In the Base it suggests the compassion should be brought to bear on any worldly problems, and if this is related to a sexual problem then it indicates that selfless love will resolve the conflict. At the Navel center it indicates that psychic transformation must be tempered by the wisdom of the Heart. Located at the Throat the Oracle indicates the ingestion of spiritual teachings, particularly through dreams or visions, developing as the faculties of visualization and concentration. At the Head center this card reveals the blissful experience of cosmic consciousness and the potential for developing an immortal point of reference outside of time-bound limitations.

45

Like a Bubble

LIKE A BUBBLE bears the number "45," signifying the path of self as related to the world of phenomena. According to the classification by elements this is a Water card, normally related to the suit of Cups in the Minor Arcana of the traditional Tarot.

The head and breasts of a reclining woman are seen partially emerging from a sea of colored waters out of which a number of bubbles ascend. The waters symbolize the many aspects and elements of the world, the reclining woman indicates the relaxed attitude needed before the bubbles of pure consciousness can arise. The diaphanous wings of the dragonfly, positioned at either side of the head, tell of the tenuous nature of all experience, life and death, the gossamer veil of illusion which shimmers like the skin on a bubble or the colored surface of the pool. The concept of the bubble of the world is mentioned in the Vedas and is a potent topic of meditation taken up in the Tantras. The bubble is a very fragile but self-contained unit, which floats upward when freed, eventually to disappear into nothingness. As an evocation of the memory of original unity, spontaneously rising, the bubble is likened to the world as a dream: "like a bubble, like a dream, thus is reality."

Divinatory Meaning

Let go of all preconceptions, open up the mind to its original and spontaneous nature. Treasure all fleeting moments of joyful ecstasy, so strengthening the potency of such experiences, yet without holding on to any form. Do not cling to the world or to its multicolored manifestations, both within and without. When this card is located at the Base center in the Tree of Life it represents the Thought of Enlightenment, as a memory from the unconscious mind. In the Heart it tells of a romantic nature coupled with a tendency not to believe in the endurance of emotions in the world, suggesting the need for faith. At the Throat it tells of insight, inspiration or a sudden moment of recall. At the Head it tells of the spirit longing for a path of teaching. Meditate on the transient nature of all phenomena.

46

Abundance

ABUNDANCE bears the number "46," signifying the fulfillment of the self in harmony with the world. According to the classification by elements this is a Water card, normally related to the suit of Cups in the Minor Arcana of the traditional Tarot.

Situated high in the mind-sky a silver chalice is depicted overflowing with gold coins. The chalice represents the self, or a position which is being offered to the self. The golden coins symbolize the inner riches, either literally or alchemically as the transformation of spiritual light. Alchemically the chalice is the hermetic vessel, formed of purest silver, representing the moon of the intellect, and the gold coming from this chalice is evocative of the inner sun of vitality, burning up all impurities and distilling the elixir of life. The image depicts a time of distribution of riches, either in the world or in the realm of the psyche, as secret teachings.

Divinatory Meaning

Rely on the capacity of the self to bring about a fortunate change in circumstances. It suggests material abundance or spiritual attainment, depending on the location of this card on the Tree of Life chart. It suggests the fulfillment of desires, particularly with reference to a question put to the Oracle. At the Base center it tells of material riches or sexual harmony, in the Spleen it relates to the digestion and utilization of earth-resources within the body, and at the Navel center the indication is of good fortune in all undertakings. When located at the Heart it suggests a wealth of emotional experience in the future, and generosity, either in the material or spiritual sense depending on the other influences. At the Throat the card shows a time of creative achievement, and in the Head center it tells of the outcome of the question. Meditate on the creative chalice.

47

Horseplay

HORSEPLAY bears the number "47," signifying the self moving along an occult path of spontaneity. According to the classification by elements this is a Water card, normally related to the suit of Cups in the Minor Arcana of the traditional Tarot.

Three white horses plunge inland across a glistening seashore, evocative of the white horses which appear as foamy crests of waves out in the ocean when swept by wind. The central horse of the group is winged, indicating that, like Pegasus, he is the messenger of the gods, carrying teachings from another dimension. The three horses symbolize fantasy as a wave of inspiration. On the wet sand an extra horse with a rider is reflected, reminiscent of the Four Horsemen of the Apocalypse, so suggesting the end of the known reality and the entry into another. In the foreground two reddish horses relate affectionately to each other, their position and color evoking the feeling of play within the heart liberated from worldly concerns, just as on the threshold of the apparent world the inner spirit plays.

Divinatory Meaning

A doorway through to the spontaneous imagination. This card suggests that fantasy is given precedence, related to the location on the Tree of Life chart. A transcendent experience or message which brings joy to the heart and lightness to the spirit. At the Base it can indicate a return to nature and the recognition of natural forces within the psyche; also to a sexual experience drawing on fantasy, opening an occult doorway. In the Spleen position it suggests, an openness to psychic forces and the need to know and strengthen the pathways of the subtle body in order to maintain equilibrium. At the Navel it tells of a lightening of pressures through the power of spontaneity. In the Heart this card tells of an uplifting of the emotions through a mystical experience, an affair based on a mystic bond. At the Throat the suggestion is of mediumistic experience, while in the Head it represents a message from the other world, or "horseplay" as the result of a worldly question.

48

White Lady: Mother of Pearl

WHITE LADY: MOTHER OF PEARL bears the number "48," signifying the projected self in a position of power. According to the classification by elements this is a Water card, normally related to the suit of Cups in the Minor Arcana of the traditional Tarot.

A white woman releases from her hand a trail of pearls which fall away down a tunnel of ice. Her belly is the inside section of a blue shell whose spiral structure indicates that she is queen of all spirals of existence and that from her womb much karma is born. She herself is beyond life and death; cold, untouchable, to be glimpsed only by those who receive her pearls, which are both wisdom and the lure which tempts mankind back into the cycles of death and rebirth Her path is not of the heart, but of the desire for rational knowledge She offers shimmering gifts to attract beings to her domain of detachment, occultism and magical acts, but once the bait is accepted her power becomes an addiction, as a muse to the poet. The White Lady uses the vital energy of her devoted followers to augment her own power, taking their fate into her own domain.

Divinatory Meaning

The person receiving this card is not a master of his or her own destiny. Such is the price paid in order to gain certain powers. The card indicates mystical inclinations and occult faculties, but this is coupled with a weakness of character, an addiction to power-giving intoxicants such as drugs, alcohol, money and so forth, at the cost of the exalted human qualities. At the Base location it suggests the use and possible misuse of intoxicants, and the separation of the sexual function from a reference point of love. In the Spleen it is a danger to health, a morbidity of assimilation; at the Navel the White Lady represents transformation itself and the ability to preserve the essence of what one has learned even past the point of death. In the Heart it shows coldness and detachment from feelings, in the Throat the card indicates the muse and in the Head, commitment is indicated. Meditate on the need to unite both head and heart to achieve liberation. Understand her as a glyph of the analytical mind.

49

Cutting Through

CUTTING THROUGH bears the number "49," signifying the full resolution of the path of the self, the occult experience linking this world to the next. According to the classification by elements this is a Water card, normally related to the suit of Cups in the Minor Arcana of the traditional Tarot.

From the waters at the base of this card there emerges a single hand which holds aloft a rope noose (with one male and one female terminal) which is symbolically used in tantric rites for binding enemies. From out of the clear sky of pure consciousness, within which clouds of thought-forms evolve, two hands appear bearing choppers. These represent the twofold nature of discriminating wisdom (the Wisdom and Means), cutting through the bonds of the cycles of death and rebirth. This whole picture thus represents the way in which the unconscious mind should be searched for the pure motivation within.

Divinatory Meaning

Act in a decisive and conclusive manner upon all problems of thought which inhibit clarity. Use Wisdom (right thinking) and Means (right action) to achieve liberation from any such problems and do not be afraid to eliminate concepts which are without any practical value. When located at the Base in the Tree of Life chart it shows a severing with past karma, a detachment from habitual traps. At the Spleen it tells of the need to be consciously aware of bodily functions, particularly with regard to physical and spiritual nourishment. In the Navel location the card suggests that a consciously willed act would effect a change of psychological position, particularly with regard to psychic transformation. At the Heart it indicates a very positive decisive situation, the fruit of discriminating wisdom, while at the Throat it foretells psychic exorcism. When this card falls in the Head location it represents a spiritual breakthrough, preparing the ground for real commitment. If in relation to a problem, it indicates resolution and attainment of goals.

50

Recall / Memory

RECALL/MEMORY bears the number "50," signifying the path of the unconscious as initiation. According to the classification by elements this is a Water card, normally related to the suit of Cups in the Minor Arcana of the traditional Tarot.

On the shores of the sky, a doorway to enlightenment, the beachcomber of the mind discovers shells among the driftwood. In the foreground is a large pink conch shell, representing the need to recall the essence of all existence, the original beginning, just as the seashell echoes the sound of the sea. The conch symbolizes the vibration of all things, for all animate and inanimate objects are comprised of particles vibrating at characteristic frequencies. The sound of the conch is used in religious ceremonies to attract higher orders of spiritual vibrations and to repel low level vibrations.

Divinatory Meaning

This is the point to stop and recollect before taking action. Remember the past in order to know how to act in the present. The card represents a moment when the vast memory within each one of us surfaces in order that we may learn from it. At the Base location the card represents the memory of a past event, reminding the questioner to relate his problems to past experience. At the Spleen it tells of the need to enliven the body functions, to lead a more physically active life. In the Navel it points to the path of least resistance in the resolution of the present situation. At the Heart it indicates that the power of sentiment is very strong and suggests that there is a feeling of longing in the heart of the questioner, which is directed back into the unconscious mind. The influence cards on the Heart location give precise indications as to the input from the unconscious mind. When situated at the Throat the card suggests that the questioner should take advice from others, while at the Head it represents nostalgia of the spirit and a processing of the past. This card is very much the glyph of the personal unconscious mind of the questioner.

51

Deep End

DEEP END bears the number "51," signifying the path of the self as related to the evolution of the psyche. According to the classification by elements this is the last, or tenth, of the Water cards, normally related to the suit of Cups in the Minor Arcana of the traditional Tarot.

A mermaid, half woman and half fish, is depicted diving deep into seemingly bottomless waters. This represents the plunge of the psyche of the seeker into the waters of the unconscious. The adaptability of the self is symbolized by the partial transformation into a fish, indicating that this is an unknown area requiring such psychic adaptability in order to make the plunge fearlessly.

Divinatory Meaning

Abandon restrictions made by the ego and let yourself go freely in the all-enveloping ocean of emotion. This represents a situation where one finds oneself in an alien environment needing adaptability. When located at the Base position in the Tree of Life chart it represents unconscious motivations and their results in the past. In the Spleen it tells of vitality-principles moving downward, suggesting that there is too much looseness in the physical and emotional areas, a nervous disposition which can be corrected by dietary discipline. In the Navel position the card denotes a need to give up strong feelings of self-centeredness in order to achieve psychic transformation through the female energy principles influencing the questioner. At the Heart it indicates an all-enveloping feeling of love and the tendency to derive psychic energy from the emotions. In the Throat it suggests that one should be prepared to accept the advice of another, while in the Head the card indicates an emotionally charged mind, probably in connection with the question, and tells of an individual deriving wisdom from the area of the intuition.

52

The Rose Garden

THE ROSE GARDEN bears the number "52," signifying the fulfillment of the path of intuition. According to the classification by elements this is the first of the Earth cards, normally related to the suit of Pentacles in the Minor Arcana of the traditional Tarot.

The card is filled with the open blossoms of various shades of pink roses. The velvety texture, delicate hues and remembered fragrance suggests the garden of earthly delights, that secret sensual place where all desires are fulfilled to abundance. With petals voluptuous and soft as open mouths, the roses represent the delight of the senses and the offering of the secrets of an inner sanctum.

Divinatory Meaning

A highly pleasurable and fulfilling experience, heightening the senses and taking a mystic position within the heart. A special secret experience where the sensual becomes the mystical. At the Base location in the Tree of Life chart it represents a passionate sexual experience and/or an earthly abundance, a life of luxury. In the Spleen it symbolizes the distilled essence of all things taken into the self, radiating health and growth. At the Navel this card indicates refined sensibility and the fruit of all transformations, whereas at the Heart it tells of emotional fulfillment and completion leading to the attainment of heart desires. In the Throat it is the image of the dream, the aspirations, in their realized form, suggesting that for the questioner the sensual and creative natures are inseparable. At the Head location the card tells of the realization of all the innermost desires as the outcome, particularly with regard to affairs of the heart. Meditate on this card as the garden of delight, the essential Nature-principle as embodied within the psyche.

53

Tree Spirit: Yakshi

TREE SPIRIT: YAKSHI bears the number "53," signifying the power path of Nature. According to the classification by elements this is an Earth card normally related to the suit of Pentacles in the Minor Arcana of the traditional Tarot.

A monkey-puzzle tree with the tree-spirit inhabiting it is pictured standing, like the Tree of Life, between the sun and moon.

The sun and moon represent the solar and lunar forces of Nature and their cycles of activity in the world as the biological rhythms. The spirit of the tree, known as Yakshi in the Indian tradition, is portrayed as a goddess or *devi,* inhabiting and ruling the tree as the vehicle of *prakriti* (the Nature principle) which is present in all worldly things. The card represents animism, the doctrine popular with those people who live and work close to the land, that all inanimate objects and natural phenomena possess a spiritual essence.

Divinatory Meaning

The solution to a problem that has been puzzling the mind of the questioner, through relating the problem to natural cycles of forces. Rid the mind of all concepts about the details of things and try to see the basic nature in its clear simplicity. When located at the Base region in the Tree of Life chart the card represents a deep understanding of Nature, for it shows a tree at the base of a larger tree, suggesting the link between the self and the natural forces. At the Spleen it shows principles of growth, the rising sap of self-knowledge. In the Navel the card shows the tree-goddess as if at the center of a maypole, evoking the feeling of transformation and psychic rebirth. At the Heart, the Tree Spirit is the embodiment of Nature in the form of the Great Illusion (Mahamaya), meaning that there is a deep need to become one with the natural order, the unity of microcosm (the self) with macrocosm (the universe which it inhabits). At the Throat location the card indicates that the problem of the questioner is in entering into communication with the Nature principle. In the Head the Tree Spirit rules the reading. This suggests that elemental forces are bearing on the reading. Meditate on the Nature principle.

54

Asylum

ASYLUM bears the number "54," signifying the path of balance as an attribute of initiation. According to the classification by elements this is an Earth card, normally related to the suit of Pentacles in the Minor Arcana of the traditional Tarot.

A unicorn nests in the boughs of a tree which overlooks a beautiful verdant field. This is an idyllic and magical place, the fairytale land in which the imagination (here symbolized by the unicorn) rests and takes refuge from the cares of the world. The unicorn represents truth and insight, at home in the garden of Mother Nature, feeling completely at peace.

Divinatory Meaning

Find a place of refuge and recuperation, free from all worldly concerns. Believe in the powers of the imagination and take up a position of contemplation with regard to any particular question or problem. Trust in the pure potency of the intuition and you will not go astray. The card suggests a feeling of well-being when left alone, away from the worldly problems. It is a magical omen of a positive order, the precise influences of which are to be determined with reference to the position of this card on the Tree of Life chart. When located at the Base region it represents a place in which one feels or has felt at home, particularly with regard to one's position in the world. In the Spleen the card points to a desire to withdraw from distractions and to adopt a position of ease so as to realize all potential growth. In the Navel, the self is seen as the place of refuge, a psychological potential of mystical potency. At the Heart the card shows that the questioner has taken refuge in the feelings and emotions and that the inner well-being is the point of balance and the powerhouse of the body. In the Throat it shows strong imaginative tendencies, an ability to live in the world of fantasy, leading to mystical experiences, while at the Head it indicates that inner peace is achieved through the power of faith.

55

Totally Bananas

TOTALLY BANANAS bears the number "55," signifying the path of psychic release. According to the classification by elements this is an Earth card, normally related to the suit of Pentacles in the Minor Arcana of the traditional Tarot.

In the center of a forest clearing stands a tree whose trunk is comprised of a large banana with the skin peeled back to reveal the fruit inside. On the tip of the banana, representing the revealed libido (the sexual energy), two figures are standing together on their heads, as if they were the fruit of the tree. These figures represent a Boschian world of fantasy, for by reversing the life-energies within the body, a new, alternative dimension opens up. It also represents a return to primitive ideals, the large banana appearing here like a totem of the ritual being enacted by the two figures.

Divinatory Meaning

The release of latent energies, but without the conscious knowledge of how to direct them. Turning the world of appearances on its head. An unconscious fantasy, the joke of existence in the realization of the ridiculous in all things. When located at the Base region in the Tree of Life chart it represents the sexual energy moving in a downward direction, the kundalini or serpent energy reversed, suggesting that the questioner has in the past been using power to exalt the ego. In the Spleen the card indicates a potential health imbalance, particularly in the prostate gland or hormonal area; at the Navel, the psychological position of liberation from the norm and a definite change of viewpoint; and in the Heart it represents confusion of emotion and the desire to be separated from conventional attitudes to love. In the Throat it indicates the relationship of the self to the environment, an attitude of fantasy, and in the Head it tells of a conscious adoption of an unconventional position.

56

Elixir Fruit/Essence

ELIXIR FRUIT/ESSENCE bears the number "56," signifying the path of the exalted senses. According to the classification by elements this is an Earth card, normally related to the suit of Pentacles in the Minor Arcana of the traditional Tarot.

Against a bed of blackberries, symbolizing the richness of the fruits of the earth, a mouth with tongue extended emerges between two peaches, representing the past and future taste-essences. The card is the symbol of the taking of ambrosia, the taste-essence of all things, the extract of each experience of the senses. It suggests that there is an organic remedy to all physical and psychological poisons and that good taste or real discrimination is the means for realizing such a faculty within the self.

Divinatory Meaning

Take the taste of all things of the world without becoming attached to them. Move toward the sweet rather than the bitter tastes of life, the fruit of all experience. When located at the Base region in the Tree of Life chart the card indicates favorable aspects in the past, telling of a new fertile ground for growth. At the Spleen it shows the absorbing of right nourishment, indicating good health. In the Navel region the card denotes the propensity to experience as much as possible, distilling the essence of the self and using such essence as a point of psychological reference. In the Heart the suggestion is of emotional discrimination, and at the Throat it tells of a receptive attitude to creative experiences. In the Head location the card shows the questioner that the answer to the question lies in the area of discrimination, particularly with regard to things of the world. Meditate on this card as symbolic of the elixir of life, the experience of all things in a single moment of pure spontaneity.

57

Temptation

TEMPTATION bears the number "57," signifying the path of occult choice. According to the classification by elements this is an Earth card, normally related to the suit of Pentacles in the Minor Arcana of the traditional Tarot.

A snake, representing the tempter or the tempted, pokes a head with extended tongue between two apples, symbolizing earthly temptation and the divine apple of cosmic knowledge. A situation is shown where a choice has to be made between two things, here depicted as identical images, mirrored aspects of each other. As it is "that what is below is as that which is above," at the same time here the snake represents the kundalini, the sexual energy, having to choose ascent (to the Head) or descent (to the Base), so invoking divine wisdom or earthly power.

Divinatory Meaning

A tempting offer, yet a decision has to be made which should be based on the highest motivations. A situation where one has the chance to gain much if the correct standpoint is maintained. When located in the Base center of the Tree of Life the card tells of sexual temptation and a past decision in relation to the world. At the Spleen it suggests an energy blockage, something needing further resolution. In the Navel it is a psychological turning point, yet requiring an immediate decision, while at the Heart it shows a lack of commitment, indecision, related to the four influence cards bearing on it. In the Throat the card relates to fantasy and the realm of the imagination, possibly telling of an initiation to come, and in the Head position the indication is that a decision has to be made and that if consideration is taken of the transcendental nature of all phenomenal things, then there will be a positive outcome; otherwise an imminent threat may come to pass. Meditate on this card as a doorway through to occult realms yet needing right action in order to progress without falling on the way.

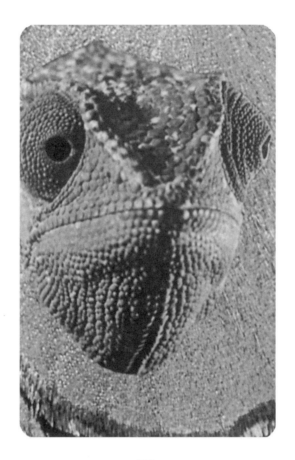

58

Chameleon

CHAMELEON bears the number "58," signifying path of adaptability. According to the classification by elements this is an Earth card, normally related to the suit of Pentacles in the Minor Arcana of the traditional Tarot.

The enormous head of a chameleon is pictured against a butterfly wing, symbolizing the ability of the developed psyche to change its coloring to suit the environment in which it is located. The suggestion is that through the wide spectrum of the chameleon's color range, he has become like the most fleeting detail of the environment, which here is the butterfly. The colored wing of the butterfly represents beauty and transience, flitting briefly in and out of life, so that the decision of the momentary color of the chameleon has no long-term value. The chameleon is most perceptive yet of limited intelligence, and is constantly alert to threats, using the faculty of adaptability as a protection from predators of the world.

Divinatory Meaning

This card tells of a person who is able to see all around a situation but is unwilling to take a risk. The position of adaptability changing always to suit the environment. It suggests that the questioner can be easily influenced and yet this is a protection from the pressures of the world. When located at the Base region in the Tree of Life chart the card indicates that the questioner has not taken a firm position in the past and that it would be good to reconsider such a stance. In the Spleen the suggestion is that it would be wise to make an actual change with regard to diet, nourishment and so forth, either materially or socially. At the Navel location it tells of an adaptable psychological position, while in the Heart it can mean a fickle nature and the need to merge with the flow of influences on the Heart in order to understand how to adapt to an emotional situation. When in the Throat region this card indicates a natural ability for fantasy, while in the Head the indication is of a real need to make a positive willful change, a positive decision.

59

Pearls Before Swine

PEARLS BEFORE SWINE bears the number "59," signifying the path of discrimination through self-awareness. According to the classification by elements this is an Earth card, normally related to the suit of Pentacles in the Minor Arcana of the traditional Tarot.

From behind a huge pile of pearls an enormous pig emerges obviously having devoured a good number of them. Traditionally pigs represent ignorance and are therefore not suitable for appreciating the pearls (symbolizing wisdom). This card is a twentieth century glyph of discrimination, warning against loss of the capacity for appreciation, if the faculty of discrimination is not exercised. It has a double meaning, also, for the pig is in its mystic aspect the symbol of the Dakini Vajravarahi, the "Diamond Sow" of discriminating wisdom, who in fact rules over all pearls of wisdom.

Divinatory Meaning

Use discrimination and do not let the sense of selfhood become inflated. Guard against disillusionment, particularly with regard to all worldly matters. Keep company with those who bring out the best rather than the worst aspects of personality. When located at the Base region in the Tree of Life chart this card indicates lack of fulfillment in the past, telling of disappointments and pointing to the need to rise above such situations in the future. At the Spleen the suggestion is of a need to discriminate with regard to all types of nourishment, in particular with respect to diet. At the Navel region the card indicates the psychological position and tells that selection and rejection should be utilized in order to achieve the most growth of character. In the Heart the card tells of emotional problems, difficulties in human relationships, which can be overcome if discriminating wisdom is brought within. At the Throat it tells of lack of appreciation and in the Head center the card advises that a choice must be made.

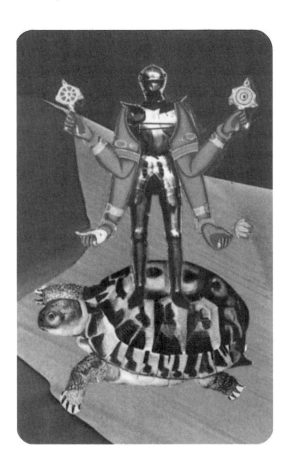

60

Taking up Arms

TAKING UP ARMS bears the number "60," signifying the accept-ance of responsibility as an expression of evolution. According to the classification by elements this is an Earth card, normally related to the suit of Pentacles in the Minor Arcana of the traditional Tarot.

Against an abstract desert, symbolizing the battle ground of eternity, a figure in armor stands upon the back of a tortoise. This figure has four arms, the upper hands of which hold two weapons (symbols of the wrathful warlike aspect) and the lower ones hold a conch and lotus, representing renewed spirituality. This form is an incarnation of Vishnu, the Hindu Lord of Preservation, in a particular aspect related to his tortoise incarnation, the symbol of evolution from the waters to the dry land. Vishnu took on different incarnations in different aeons in order to overcome various demons who had been troubling the world and the gods. Here this form is evoked to represent a position of great strength, taken on to overcome all adversity both in this world and the next.

Divinatory Meaning

Fearlessness, the adoption of a position of strength, particularly with regard to a question put to the Oracle. It suggests the need to protect the essence of the self against any outside attacks, so to maintain one's real integrity. When located in the Base region of the Tree of Life chart this card indicates that one has not had things easy and that the questioner should still take care to protect the self from attacks, particularly in the area of worldly situations. In the Spleen location the card tells of a tightening of the subtle body, through self-discipline, so cutting off all entry points for malignant forces to enter. At the Navel it indicates invulnerability; in the Heart location the card indicates the strength of emotional commitment. In the Throat the suggestion is a mystic position of power, and in the Head center it tells of a firm Will, bringing real results through standing firm to one's principles.

61

Survival

SURVIVAL bears the number "61," signifying unity within the self, as related to the world. According to the classification by elements this is the last, or tenth, of the Earth cards, normally related to the suit of Pentacles in the Minor Arcana of the traditional Tarot.

Great slag heaps form hills of the landscape. On the horizon factory chimneys belch polluting smoke into the sky, yet in the foreground a few green shoots manage to push upward from the unlikely soil. This represents the survival of the life-force, manifesting itself even in the most difficult environment. The slag heaps and smoking chimneys represent the misuse of the natural world by urban society, presenting us with a picture of pollution in action in the modern world.

Divinatory Meaning

The situation portrayed by the card is the instinct to survive. The pollution may be in one's domicile or even in the mind itself, yet within both there is the potent desire to survive at all costs. The indication is that the positive will always triumph, whatever the odds, and that this realization even in appalling situations is itself the seed of the cure. When located in the Base center of the Tree of Life chart this card usually represents one's actual worldly environment, particularly as related to the past, and warns of dangers from unhealthy sexual encounters. At the Spleen it tells of the body being overworked and suggests the need for care with respect to health. In the Navel position the card indicates that the questioner should search inside and be careful to preserve only that part of the self worth keeping and transforming; there is also an indication of some polluting influence acting on the psyche, possibly through a hypocritical attitude of a so-called friend. At the Heart it shows difficulty in the area of emotions, with transformation needed as indicated by the four influence cards. In the Throat it is an indication of bad advice having been given, and in the Head it tells of the need for the power of faith to triumph over all polluting obstacles.

62

Dangerous Pussy / The Past

DANGEROUS PUSSY/THE PAST bears the number "62," signifying the occult transmission of power as gnosis. According to the cycle of activity of *The Tantric Dakini Oracle* this card indicates the potent power of the past.

The face of a lioness fills the card, looking out with sultry eyes, between which a lion sits with paws outstretched, emerging from a mane formed by a cascade of blond human hair. This card evokes the seductive and dangerous aspects of the raw female energy, depicted as the dangerous pussy of our pack. In her mystical form of Senge Dolma, the lionheaded savioress, she is the dakini of Padmasambhava, the holder of the tantric teachings who brought the transmission to Tibet. In such an aspect she is the guardian of the deck, the initiation card into *The Tantric Dakini Oracle*. This card is the Past, indicating that the power is such that it has been able to protect the tantric secrets throughout all the ages.

Divinatory Meaning

This is the high potency point of entry into the occult transmission, a protector to those who value absolute truth and a ruthless destroyer of those who deny it. The person receiving this card should take it as a potent initiation and examine the heart, so as to be ready for sudden insights. In all locations on the Tree of Life chart this card should be understood as a potent invocation of the past, particularly with regard to the tantric left-hand path, which stresses that there should be no hesitation to perform potent acts provided one is prepared to handle the consequences. It is an indication of a position of power and responsibility, an occult transmission from the past extending into the present. If in the Base region, it relates to sexuality; in the Navel it suggests dramatic changes; in the Heart, a mystic initiation; and in the Head the suggestion is of a new potent experience.

63

Centering / The Present

CENTERING/THE PRESENT bears the number "63," signifying the power of the triple nature pervading all things and becoming a glyph of the essence of the inner and outer realities. According to the cycle of activity of *The Tantric Dakini Oracle* this card indicates the potent power of the present.

A mandala of the self, the Sri Chakra, is pictured across the surface of the moon, the blue color of which emphasizes the cooling nature of this source of wisdom. The Sri Chakra consists of combined male and female energy aspects manifesting as five ascending and four descending triangles respectively, forming forty-three triangles in total, signifying the integration of the inner and outer worlds, microcosm with macrocosm. Each of the triangles contains small figures of deities, reminding us that all the gods exist within each one of us, as the exalted attributes of the psyche. Around the figure created by the triangles there is an inner red and outer white circular lotus enclosure, representing the combined self-created female and male essence-principles respectively, out of which all things are formed. This card depicts the eternal present, the spontaneous nonduality of the moment outside of time-limitations. It is an initiation into this understanding.

Divinatory Meaning

Concentration on the potency of living in the present. An understanding of the self's position outside of time coming through spiritual practices and the developed intuition. At the Base region in the Tree of Life chart this card shows that by centering on past problems to do with the world, the power of transcendence will be brought into the present. In the Spleen it tells of growth, at the Navel the indication is of developed concentration, a psychological power point of high potency. At the Heart the Oracle tells of fulfillment and in the Head there is a strong indication of the achievement of desires in the present through the power of the cooling lunar wisdom-essence. This card is always positive, a teaching of the absolute truth of the eternal present.

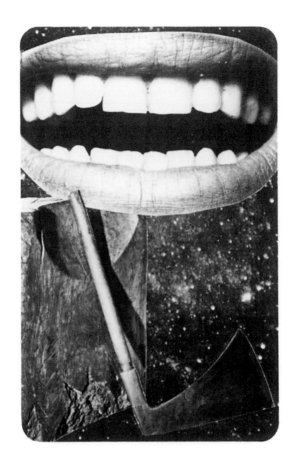

64

The Last Laugh/The Future

THE LAST LAUGH/THE FUTURE bears the number "64," signifying the exalted cycle of transformation of the psyche, the number of the Secret Dakinis. According to the cycle of activity of *The Tantric Dakini Oracle,* this card indicates the potent power of the future.

The chopping block and axe of an executioner are depicted as the final outpost on the brink of eternity, symbolized by the night sky behind. A gigantic disembodied laughing mouth rises above the implement of execution, symbolizing the spirit liberated by its own humor. The card represents the great cosmic joke of recurring birth and death, the cycles of existence, pointing out that the spirit outlives the body and so is automatically freed from the snares of fate and destiny once it takes a transcendent position. The mouth laughing in ecstasy is the symbol of mahamaya, the Great Illusion, laughing at the play of existence and at all the things which we take so seriously. As the sixty-fourth card of the deck, it is related to the Joker around which *The Tantric Dakini Oracle* cards are dancing as expressions of the psyche of the questioner. This card represents the Future through the glyph of the laughing higher Self, which suggests that destiny is really in the hands of the self.

Divinatory Meaning

Take a position of ascendancy in the present situation and all obstacles will be overcome. See the humor in all situations, rather than taking life too seriously. Even morbidity is only a state of mind. Learn to laugh at yourself and at the situations you find yourself in and in doing so, cut through all limitations normally attributed to karma. Free yourself from attachments. When located at the Base center in the Tree of Life chart it represents the need to detach from worldly ambition and to understand past and future as one, thereby taking control over one's own destiny. At the Navel the card tells of ruthless self-work, but with humor so bringing about a psychological breakthrough; in the Heart it tells of the desire for emotional liberation through humor, and in the Head it tells of an advantage gained.

PART IV:

Readings

$\mathcal{S}$ample I

Peter, movie-maker and multi-media artist, thirties, currently trying to put together a new commercial packaged program for tour, but without having to make too many artistic compromises. A very talented and dynamic personality, who finds it difficult to work with others. He complains of periods of depression, attributing them to pressures of ideals, coupled with an unresolved emotional involvement going back years. The question put to *The Tantric Dakini Oracle* asked to know the "price" of success, with regard to the new project and the problems of ideals with regard to emotional and spiritual ties.

Traditional Tarot Method—The Celtic Cross

Figure 5 illustrates the Tarot meanings that apply to the positions in a traditional Celtic Cross layout.

First place, signifying the "general situation" surrounding the question, card 50, RECALL/MEMORY, a Water suit. This card indicates that the unconscious must be brought to the surface, for it contains within it all the clues that are of direct relevance to this consultation. The suggestion is that the experiences of the past will help to show a clear way through the dilemmas of the present.

Second place, crossing the first card and signifying the "opposing force," card 32, SHIVA: THE PILLAR OF FIRE, a Fire suit. This card indicates that there is a great dynamic drive working through

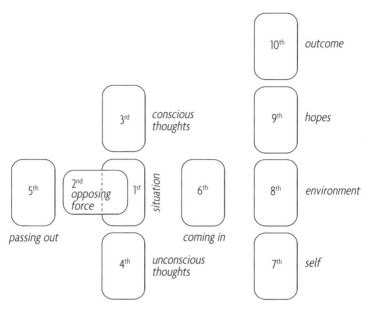

Figure 5. Celtic Cross Layout

the questioner. This may be even too strong, needing to be converted from its raw energy aspect to a subtler astral light. The inner fire, when refined, can totally transform the personality. On the other hand, if it is not controlled it can create havoc in the whole being.

Third place, signifying the "conscious thoughts" on the matter, card 29, SELF-PRESERVATION, an Air suit. This card indicates the need to withdraw into and protect the self in order to preserve timeless values.

Fourth place, signifying the "unconscious thoughts" on the matter, card 18, SOMA, of the Major Arcana group and related to the Moon of the traditional Tarot. This card tells of the entry of higher spiritual forces into the unconscious, thereby raising the level of intuition, insight and imagination. A very positive card, especially to do with spiritual creativity.

Fifth place, signifying what is "passing out" or has passed, card 60, TAKING UP ARMS, an Earth suit. This indicates that the position

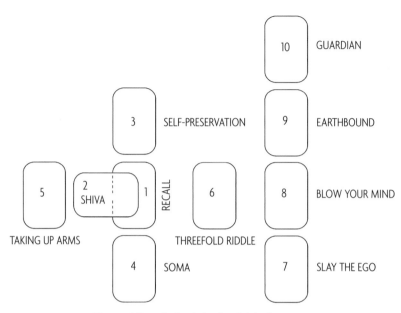

Figure 6. Peter's Cards in the Celtic Cross

of great responsibility, needing extreme self-discipline, as experienced by the questioner in the past, will now be resolved.

Sixth place, signifying what is "coming in" to the questioner's life, card 25, THREEFOLD RIDDLE, an Air suit. This indicates an unconscious or concealed part of the self, needing resolution and requiring discrimination, for temptation will be involved. This is a very personal card, fathomed only by those who are able to search deep within themselves for the answer. It is concerned with choice.

Seventh place, signifying "the self," card 12, SLAY THE EGO, of the Major Arcana group and related to the Hanged Man of the traditional Tarot. This indicates great strength inherent in the personality. It tells of the need to surrender to a new situation without falling into the traps set up by patterns of self-aggrandizement. This suggests the need for humility as the key to selfless action. In this way the "Riddle" card will be resolved.

Eighth place, signifying "the environment," card 40, BLOW YOUR MIND, a Fire suit. This indicates that the position in which the questioner finds himself necessitates spontaneous action, freed from habitual patterns requiring the flexibility of the self as indicated by the previous card. This card indicates the potential for a major change of viewpoint, a breakthrough.

Ninth place, signifying the "hopes and expectations" of the questioner, card 21, EARTHBOUND, of the Major Arcana group and related to the World of the traditional Tarot. This indicates that the question is directed toward the worldly cycles, particularly to do with karma, with indications that there is a strong desire to change residence or country of work. It also suggests the need for new developments to emerge from out of the old ground.

Tenth place, the final location and "outcome" of the reading, card 36, GUARDIAN, a Fire suit. This indicates the burning up of all illusion and confirms the presence of a spiritual guide or guardian. This suggests that the correct application of the self of the questioner to the tasks at hand will result in the fruitful completion of the project, so laying the ground for further developments under some spiritual guidance.

A brief look back into the composition of the reading, made up of ten cards, reveals that there is a preponderance of Fire cards (three in total) and Major Arcana cards (also three), telling of a dynamic fire-like personality requiring correct channeling of the energies. The rest of the cards are in the proportion of two Air to one Water and one Earth, indicating that the real way to resolve the question is through the power (or Fire) of the psyche, used for conscious transformation (as is suggested by the same number of Major Arcana cards). The consultation indicates that discrimination is a major factor in the success of Peter's projects.

For those people interested in obtaining a numerological reading the numbers on the individual cards may be added together and used according to a system. Thus, for the above reading, we add the numbers 50, 32, 29, 18, 60, 25, 12, 40, 21 and 36, which makes a total of 324. These three numbers may then be added together, 3 + 2 + 4 = 9, the overall number of the reading. The number nine indicates psychic resolution, the completion of a cycle, the Ennead or group of nine being an occult truth of great potential, the number of the microcosm as a spiritual vehicle. This suggests that the dynamics of the reading relate to the completion of a cycle and the beginning of another, the way through to a new dimension of fulfillment. In the numerology of *The Tantric Dakini Oracle,* the number nine is related to a card entitled WAY THROUGH, the key to the Universe.

Transfer to Tree of Life Chart

The same cards drawn for the Celtic Cross traditional Tarot reading can now be transposed for a Tree of Life reading.

The cards are rotated, as in Figure 7, and placed on the Tree of Life chart, as in Figure 8 on page 174, in order to give an overall picture with respect to the subtle body and to enable a full diagno-

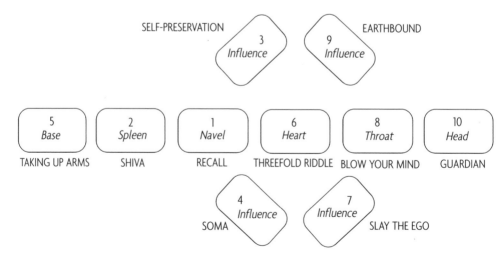

Figure 7. Peter's Rotated Cards

sis. On the Tree of Life chart the Base card is located at the bottom, with the other centers ascending into the subtle realms.

Base region, card 60, TAKING UP ARMS. This indicates that the questioner has not had things easily in the past and has often needed to protect himself in worldly situations. He has repeatedly accepted a position of too great responsibility and this is something to be transcended. The indication is that, since this card falls in the "passing out" aspect of the reading, there may be a resolution of this in the future. (This is very relevant to Peter's life, since, in the past, he has repeatedly been taken advantage of, particularly with regard to his creative projects.)

Spleen region, is card 32, SHIVA: THE PILLAR OF FIRE. This indicates that, despite psychic and material attacks, the spirit of the questioner has remained intact. This is in the "opposing force" aspect of the reading, pointing to the fact that his dynamic vital fire has enabled him to burn up negativity. The Spleen location suggests good health, particularly in the digestive functions of assimilation. However, this inner fire must become refined; otherwise, it may produce obscuration of the psyche.

Navel region, card 50, RECALL/MEMORY. This indicates that clarity on past situations will assist all transformations in the present. This card has fallen in the "situation surrounding" the questioner location, pointing to the fact that he should recall and remember where things went wrong with previous partnerships and projects, so as not to make the same mistakes again. In particular this is the line of least resistance to produce full resolution of the present situation.

Heart region, card 25, THREEFOLD RIDDLE. This indicates that his problems have essentially to do with the "emotional area" and that it is here that Peter should look for the solution to his feelings of depression or frustration. A direct examination of the Heart is required, concealing nothing and sincerely desiring real discrimination. An emotional direction is needed. The four influence cards

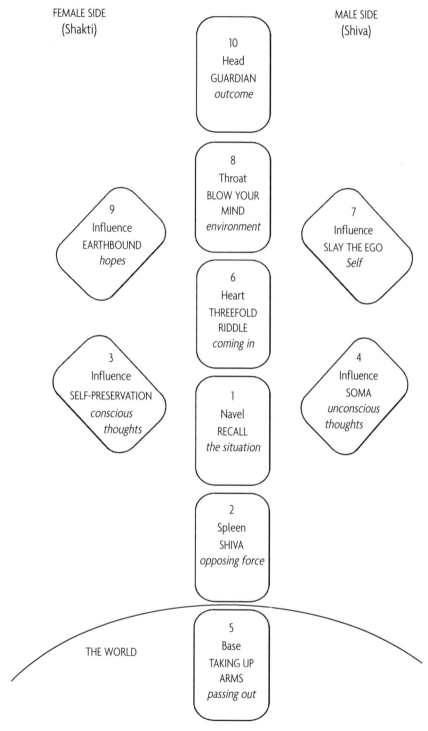

FEMALE SIDE
(Shakti)

MALE SIDE
(Shiva)

10
Head
GUARDIAN
outcome

8
Throat
BLOW YOUR
MIND
environment

9
Influence
EARTHBOUND
hopes

7
Influence
SLAY THE EGO
Self

6
Heart
THREEFOLD
RIDDLE
coming in

3
Influence
SELF-PRESERVATION
*conscious
thoughts*

1
Navel
RECALL
the situation

4
Influence
SOMA
*unconscious
thoughts*

2
Spleen
SHIVA
opposing force

THE WORLD

5
Base
TAKING UP
ARMS
passing out

Figure 8. Peter's Cards on the Tree of Life Chart

on the Heart are in complete balance, suggesting that the resolution is in fact already there, but the self must recognize and act with the wisdom of discrimination.

The four influence cards are, in this reading, complementary pairs, a healthy omen indicating a potent position for psychic transformation. The complementaries are card 29, SELF-PRESERVATION (in the place of "conscious thoughts," located in the shakti or female side of the Tree of Life), and card 12, SLAY THE EGO (in the place of "self," located in the shiva or male side of the Tree of Life). This first pair shows a balanced attitude toward preserving the timeless aesthetic while becoming egoless in the process. The second pair of complementaries are card 21, EARTHBOUND (in the place of "hopes and expectations," located in the shakti or female side of the Tree of Life), and card 18, SOMA (in the place of "unconscious thoughts," located in the shiva or male side of the Tree of Life). This second pair shows the inclination of the spirit of the questioner toward mystical illumination and wisdom coupled with the desire to manifest this on the earth.

The four influences acting on the THREEFOLD RIDDLE card at the Heart location may prove to be of great help to Peter in understanding his emotional problems. The fact that the cards are in a state of balance indicates a strong possibility of resolving the "riddle" through conscious self-work, using these psychological aspects as meditation keys for an emotional transformation.

Throat region, card 40, BLOW YOUR MIND. This indicates that Peter should use any method available to him to open up new channels of the mind, so as to tune in to the collective consciousness. In that this card has fallen in the "environment" location, it suggests that his work will benefit from this new approach: a sudden move toward acting totally spontaneously, without reference to predictable patterns of behavior. In this way, in his work, he will transcend the personal standpoint and produce symbols of archetypal importance.

Head region, card 36, GUARDIAN. This indicates that the projects can find their fulfillment and that for further development the direction lies in connecting with the occult lineage. Thus will he receive the teachings and be protected from worldly obstacles. For Peter this has relevance since he is inclined in this direction and needs the guiding and protecting force to help eliminate worldly difficulties and to add significance to his creative energy. However, the THREEFOLD RIDDLE card at the Heart location indicates an urgent need for emotional maturity, without which his GUARDIAN card cannot work effectively. The reading suggests that a sexual-emotional problem is in need of resolution and once it is cleared there will be a real opportunity for evolution along artistic and spiritual directions.

Sample II

Bhagawan, spiritual seeker, traveler, singer, yogi, mid-thirties, spent some years in India with teacher practicing yoga and tantra philosophy. Returned to America accompanied by wife. Following birth of child, tours, and concerts went through a period of depression with emotional problems. Then remarriage, birth of child, move to the city, recording spiritual songs, frustration with worldly problems, longing to return to a natural environment. On the day of the reading he expressed great desire to reestablish the tantric way of life. His question related to the events of the coming summer, and in particular to an impending move away from the city.

His wife, four months pregnant, was present and also requested a reading, which follows and is our SAMPLE III. Readings for a couple made at the same time often give particularly clear indications of the events of the past and lead to advice for the future.

Traditional Tarot Method—The Celtic Cross

Figure 9 shows the cards Bhagawan drew for each position.

First place, signifying the "general situation" surrounding the question, card 13, DEATH/TRANSFIGURATION, of the Major Arcana group and related to the Death card of the traditional Tarot. This card indicates the breaking of ties, a drastic change. Since the questioner had in mind an immediate departure from the city, a complete uprooting of the last two years, this seems particularly appropriate and

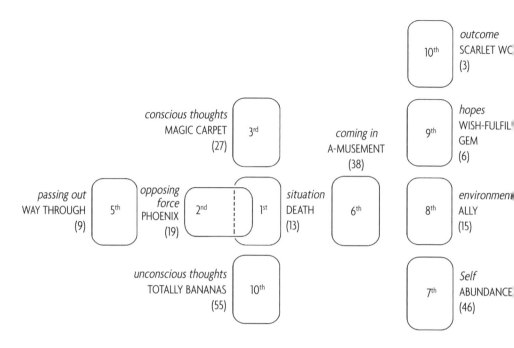

Figure 9. Bhagawan's Cards in the Celtic Cross

suggests that this move will be fruitful, especially with regard to the worldliness of his present situation, which he wishes to transcend.

Second place, crossing the first card and signifying the "opposing force," card 19, PHOENIX, of the Major Arcana group and related to the Sun of the traditional Tarot. This card indicates spiritual rebirth, portrayed as the Cosmic Couple rising out of the ashes of the old world. It is a very positive card in this place since it represents the spiritual love which the questioner finds hard to contact in the world of responsibility, particularly as regards the family.

Third place, signifying the "conscious thoughts" on the matter, card 27, MAGIC CARPET, an Air suit. This card indicates a strong desire not to be bound up by the physical world and its habitual patterns. It is a desire for "transport" in every sense of the term, both in the physical world (through a change of residence, travel) and in the spirit. The four figures on the corners of the Magic Carpet are in the same male/female form as the Cosmic Couple in the previous Phoenix card, indicating that it is the reborn and unified self which the questioner wishes to become.

Fourth place, signifying the "unconscious thoughts" on the matter, card 55, TOTALLY BANANAS, an Earth suit. This card suggests that the unconscious thoughts surrounding the question are as yet scrambled and confused, but that the positive motivation will help to turn the world of appearance on its head. It indicates a return to nature and to primitive expression, unrestricted by convention.

Fifth place, signifying what is "passing out" or has passed, card 9, WAY THROUGH, of the Major Arcana group and related to the Hermit of the traditional Tarot. This indicates that the questioner has been given direction and guidance in the past and that a cycle has in effect been completed.

Sixth place, signifying what is "coming in" to the questioner's life, card 38, A-MUSEMENT, a Fire suit. This card is related to the occult path of fulfillment through recognition of the female power-principle (shakti), the muse, and the enjoyment and release to be experienced. It could also indicate an affair, or the left-hand tantric lifestyle.

Seventh place, signifying "the self," card 46, ABUNDANCE, a Water suit. In this place the card tells of the riches of the self. It also can imply that material worries will be resolved. This is a very positive card, pointing to alchemical transformation.

Eighth place, signifing "the environment," card 15, ALLY, of the Major Arcana group and related to the Devil card of the traditional Tarot. In this position the indication is clearly that the questioner needs to overcome the downward moving or negative aspects of the outside world, the city lifestyle in particular, and that this will come about through eliminating destructive aspects of the psyche.

Ninth place, signifying the "hopes and expectations" of the questioner, card 6, WISH-FULFILLING GEM, of the Major Arcana group and related to the Lovers of the traditional Tarot. This is a highly auspicious and fortunate card, telling of the desire for fulfillment and indicating that such is within reach. The return of good fortune, leading to divine love, the All-Good Buddha.

Tenth place, the final location and the "outcome" of the reading, card 3, SCARLET WOMAN, of the Major Arcana group and related to the Empress of the traditional Tarot. This indicates the manifestation of the female principle, the shakti or energy, the female counterpart for divine union. In the world it tells of the questioner being concerned with the pregnancy of his wife; "out of the world" it tells of the combination of spiritual practice *(bhakti)* and the archetypal female energy (shakti). There is a strong indication that the questioner is aware of the tantric path of female energy (shakti) and its power of transformation.

A brief look back into the composition of the reading, made up of ten cards, reveals that there is one card for each of the four main elements, Earth, Air, Water and Fire, and that the remainder are all Major Arcana cards. This in particular indicates a strong reading, well balanced and with the future indications clear.

The numerological position is obtained by adding together the numbers on the individual cards. In the above reading, 13, 19, 27, 55, 9, 38, 46, 15, 6 and 3 make a total of 231. These three numbers are then added together: 2 + 3 + 1 = 6, the overall number of the reading. The number six indicates harmony, balance, the spiritual fulfillment. In the numerology of *The Tantric Dakini Oracle* the number six is related to a card entitled WISH-FULFILLING GEM, the main boon card of the deck, indicating that the wishes of the questioner will ultimately be fulfilled. In particular, there is a suggestion of the Divine Couple, the tantric path, the archetypal ancestor of the human spirit.

Transfer to Tree of Life Chart

Base region, card 9, WAY THROUGH. This indicates that for the questioner the key to the mysteries is to be found in the world through the completion of natural cycles of activity, particularly with regard to karma. The key of the universe, as depicted by this card, suggests ascent upward through the subtle yoga body, producing phenomena at every center. Here it also represents the guidance of a spiritual teacher (in the past), manifested on earth and related to the invocation of Ganesh, the elephant-headed Lord of Obstacles, who rules the Base region. (This is relevant to Bhagawan's reading, since his teacher passed away some years ago.)

Spleen region, card 19, PHOENIX. This is, in the location, a depiction of the digestive fire, indicating that the health is not in immediate danger and pointing to the ability to burn up the dross of worldly experiences. It is a very positive card, particularly in this location, indicating that the questioner is not rooted in the world, but is consciously aware of the ascending nature of such a position. The Spleen region is where the upward moving forces from the Base (the WAY THROUGH card, in this reading) mix and unite with the downward part of the Navel (the DEATH/TRANSFIGURATION card, in this reading) producing a substance suitable for the body to digest and grow from. It is telling of a spiritual awareness born out of the ashes of the transitory world. This card is related to the Sun of the traditional Tarot.

Navel region, card 13, DEATH/TRANSFIGURATION. The influence of this card in the Solar Plexus position tells of psychological transfiguration, the end of the old self and the potential for the new. The Navel is the transformation center, where the sixty-four dakinis can dance in their play. This card here indicates that the direction in which the radiant energy of the subtle body will be pointed is toward spiritual illumination (portrayed by the light behind the head of Death), recognizable in the egoless state which

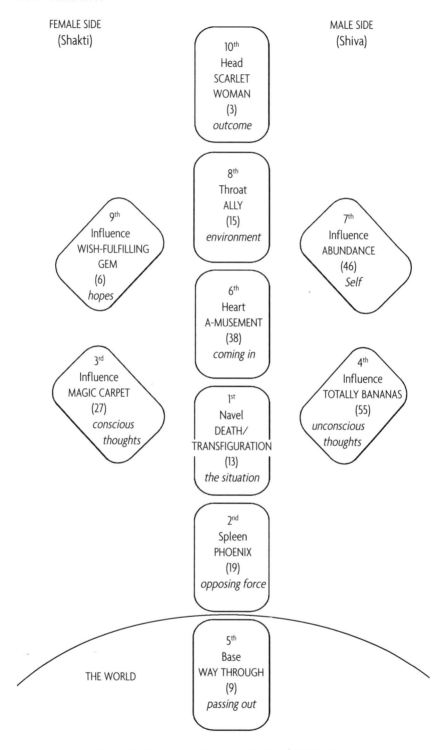

FEMALE SIDE
(Shakti)

MALE SIDE
(Shiva)

10th
Head
SCARLET
WOMAN
(3)
outcome

8th
Throat
ALLY
(15)
environment

9th
Influence
WISH-FULFILLING
GEM
(6)
hopes

7th
Influence
ABUNDANCE
(46)
Self

6th
Heart
A-MUSEMENT
(38)
coming in

3rd
Influence
MAGIC CARPET
(27)
*conscious
thoughts*

4th
Influence
TOTALLY BANANAS
(55)
*unconscious
thoughts*

1st
Navel
DEATH/
TRANSFIGURATION
(13)
the situation

2nd
Spleen
PHOENIX
(19)
opposing force

THE WORLD

5th
Base
WAY THROUGH
(9)
passing out

Figure 10. Bhagawan's Cards on the Tree of Life Chart

is beyond temporal limitations. The state of limbo in which the questioner found himself at the time of the reading suggested that the Death/Transfiguration card was particularly relevant here, pointing to a complete change of outlook, a new life, through the burning up of karma.

Heart region, card 38, A-MUSEMENT. This points to the recognition and acceptance of the shakti or female principle as the real powerhouse for the questioner. It is through his appreciation and understanding of the female energy factors that his emotions are nourished. The card suggests that the position taken within the Heart is of the emotions channeled through ritualistic rather than conventional activity. The card depicts the goddess in her various forms, together with her attendants, offering pleasure and fulfillment. The muse in the heart, divine intoxication, a fruitful moment of great potential. This is in particular the left-hand path of tantra, which has been practiced by the questioner and is therefore most relevant.

The four influence cards, bearing on the Heart, are always considered in pairs, related diagonally. Thus we have card 6, WISH-FULFILLING GEM (on the shakti side, the mystic unity) and card 55, TOTALLY BANANAS (on the shiva side, telling of his unconventionality) as one pair. Similarly we have card 46, ABUNDANCE (on the Shiva side, telling of the inner riches) and card 27, MAGIC CARPET (on the shakti side, meaning transport and delight) as the other pair. It can be seen that the questioner is particularly able to function on the shakti side, as is also suggested by other cards of the whole reading, but that the shiva aspect is as yet unresolved (as is suggested by card 55, Totally Bananas). Overall it is to be stressed that the shakti side of the Tree of Life represents the influences that the questioner is receptive to, here Wish-Fulfilling Gem and Magic Carpet. The shiva side tells of the assertive position taken by the psyche, here expressed by the card Abundance (indicating desire for spiritual or material wealth) and the card Totally Bananas (telling of unconventionality). The message of the four influences on the Heart in our reading tells of appreciation of the female essence channeled toward realization of the non-dual nature of divine union with the goddess (the anima of the psyche) and the resultant emanations of peace and compassion, a definite position of commitment to send the erotic energy toward the mystic without compromise, leading to the fulfillment of all wishes.

Throat region, card 15, ALLY. This card points to the raw power of the unconscious, particularly as related to the dream or visionary experiences. Here the depiction is of a powerful demon, in fact a guardian of the inner mandala, or mystic circle of protection. It tells of the need to complete and organize all realities, both in the world and out of it, and indicates that the Ally is at hand and ready to help overcome obstacles. This card in this location has particular relevance to the questioner, who has taken upon himself the tantric path of action, requiring real intent in order to be truly magical and potent. The Ally can be understood as a mystic form of the teacher, and in this sense it could be appropriate here, as a guardian.

Head region, card 3, SCARLET WOMAN. This position gives the "outcome" of the reading, the answer to the question put to *The Tantric Dakini Oracle*. The card which falls here is a representation of the tantric mother goddess, Kali, the exalted female energy principle, related to the Empress card of the traditional Tarot. It tells of a strongly passionate nature here expressed as the vision of the goddess, the creative principle. Since this card is connected also with birth and pregnancy it indicates that the questioner need not be concerned or unduly worried about his wife's expected child, since it is already in the position of fulfillment.

This reading can readily be summarized since its message is very clear. The indication is to maintain transcendent wisdom (the key) through correct practices, burning up and transcending the habits of the world and the defects of the gross physical body. As the shakti-principle is of central importance to the questioner he should take care to honor her correctly, letting her assume the highest rather than the worldly position. He should not doubt the intrinsic capability of the self, particularly since the Ally is ready to help and the influence of the WISH-FULFILLING GEM is already bearing on his heart. There is a real suggestion of the resolution of his problems in the coming summer, mainly through keeping contact with the spiritual path and recognizing the high potency of the creative principle, which he should see as embodied in all women. Since the questioner was already advanced along the tantric path of practice these observations seem to be of direct relevance.

Next there follows a reading, made directly onto the Tree of Life chart, for his pregnant wife who asks about the outcome of her immediate concern.

 # $\mathcal{S}$ample III

Devi, spiritual seeker, mother, twenties, one child already and another on the way. Wife of Bhagawan (whose reading was our Sample II), somewhat worried about the course of events in the future since the family is about to uproot from the city and move west to a more natural lifestyle. Also some concern about the pregnancy.

Direct Reading onto Tree of Life Chart

Base region, card 22, MOTHER'S MILK. This placement designates what is "passing out" or has passed, and is in the place of the world. The number of this card signifies a combination of the essential mother-principles of attachment and nourishment. According to the classification by elements this is an Air card, normally related to the suit of swords in the traditional Tarot Minor Arcana. It represents the aspiration for non-duality and in a literal sense it here relates to the fact that the questioner, at the time of the reading, had just stopped breast-feeding her first child, yet is aware of another child on the way.

Spleen region, card 32, SHIVA: THE PILLAR OF FIRE. This is in the position of "opposing forces," for better or worse, crossing the first card of the reading (which is the Navel card, a description of which follows). The number of this card signifies the astral light coming from the fulfillment of spiritual ideals. According to the classification by elements this is a Fire card, normally related to the suit of Wands in the Minor Arcana of the traditional Tarot. This card in particular is connected to the masculine principle of creativity, the

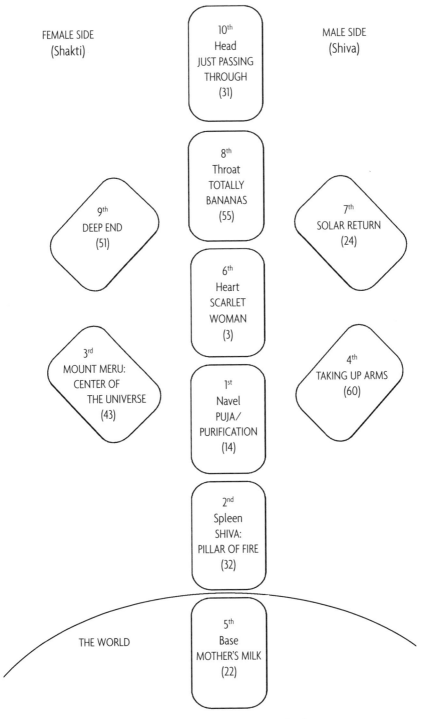

FEMALE SIDE
(Shakti)

MALE SIDE
(Shiva)

10th
Head
JUST PASSING
THROUGH
(31)

8th
Throat
TOTALLY
BANANAS
(55)

9th
DEEP END
(51)

7th
SOLAR RETURN
(24)

6th
Heart
SCARLET
WOMAN
(3)

3rd
MOUNT MERU:
CENTER OF
THE UNIVERSE
(43)

1st
Navel
PUJA/
PURIFICATION
(14)

4th
TAKING UP ARMS
(60)

2nd
Spleen
SHIVA:
PILLAR OF FIRE
(32)

THE WORLD

5th
Base
MOTHER'S MILK
(22)

Figure 11. Devi's Cards on the Tree of Life Chart

impregnator of the world to come, here understood as the pregnancy itself. At this center it tells of a healthy constitution and points to possibilities of real spiritual growth.

Navel region, card 14, PUJA/PURIFICATION. This location signifies the general "situation surrounding" the question and at this center relates to the process of transformation. The number of this card signifies mental foundation and the completion of a cosmic creative cycle. It relates to the Tarot card, Temperance, of the Major Arcana. The indication here is that the menial attitude at the time of consultation is one of dedication and humility, purifying the self to be a fit vehicle for spirituality. The card depicts a priest pouring water over a phallus, as an offering. This is the symbol of devotion, to the spiritual path, to the higher aspect of the Divine Couple.

Heart region, card 3, SCARLET WOMAN, signifying in this position what is "coming into" the life of the questioner. The number of this card tells of the threefold nature of existence (as Creation, Maintenance and Dissolution), the three times of Past, Present and Future. This card relates to the Tarot card, The Empress, of the Major Arcana. The indication here is of fecundity, the creative aspect of feminity, a Heart card, representing the resolution of divisions between spirit and body. This card is a particularly strong indication of the potent pregnant situation of the questioner, and represents a strong affirmation that this will lead to fulfillment.

The four influence cards on the Heart position should be considered as pairs to clarify their meaning. Consider card 51, DEEP END, which is a Water card. This is in the position of "hopes and expectations," signifying that the questioner wishes to find herself in a situation of unconditional surrender (such as is experienced at the birth of a child), resulting in psychic evolution. The pair of this is card 60, TAKING UP ARMS, which is an Earth card. This is the position of "unconscious thoughts," and tells of the questioner taking a protective steadfast position to safeguard herself against outside influences. She is determined not to be undermined and will protect herself from any emotional or environmental onslaught. The other pair of Influence cards are: card 24, SOLAR RETURN, an Air card, in the position of the self. This means that astrological influences are of great importance for the questioner, particularly in relation to her question about the coming baby and pointing to the acceptance of destiny as cycles of activity, leading to return to the original concept. The counterpart of this position is card 43, MOUNT MERU: CENTER OF THE UNIVERSE, in the position of "conscious thoughts." This is a Water card and tells of the integration of inner and outer worlds, in this case the recognition of the universe within, as the child to come. All the four Influence cards together point to fulfillment and development through the new experience of birth, consciously understood.

Throat region, card 55, TOTALLY BANANAS. This is in the position of the "environment," signifying the path of psychic release. This is an Earth card normally related to the suit of Pentacles in the Minor Arcana of the traditional Tarot. This card is in particular associated with unconventionality and at the Throat center of the Tree of Life tells of the relationship of the self to the environment, attitudes of fantasy or imagination. The Boschian image is relevant to the questioner since she tells of feeling totally turned around by the world and its values. This is clearly indicated by the card, the indication being that the change of environment will change things for the better.

Head region, card 31, JUST PASSING THROUGH. This is in the position of the "outcome" of the question put to *The Tantric Dakini Oracle*. This card signifies the recognition of the principles of trinity and unity combined together as the expression of the fundamental truth of worldly existence (that one is in fact just passing through this world). This is the last of the Air cards, normally related to the suit of Swords in the Minor Arcana of the traditional Tarot. This card tells of the natural inclination towards higher consciousness as the outcome of life itself. It suggests that the change of location and the birth of the new child will, for the questioner, be just further aspects of the transcendental nature of worldly existence, and that she will come to understand this as the truth of life itself.

The numerology of the reading can be determined by adding together the numbers of all the ten cards making up the reading. Thus we have 14 + 32 + 43 + 60 + 22 + 3 + 24 + 55 + 51 + 31 = 335. These three numbers may then be added together, 3 + 3 + 5 = 11, the overall number of the reading. The number eleven indicates the integration of unity as recognition of the principle of self-creation. It is the number of a new beginning which seems particularly relevant to the questioner in this reading, since she is in fact attempting to do just this by moving out of the city and also in her position as a mother about to give birth to a new child. In the numerology of *The Tantric Dakini Oracle* the number eleven is related to the card SELF-CREATED, which tells of the triumph of love and its power in the spiritual realms.

A brief look back into the composition of this reading shows that there are two Major Arcana cards, one Fire, three Air, two Water and two Earth cards, with all the elements represented. This is an indication of the state of psychic balance of the questioner.

It is interesting that when this reading is compared to the previous one (Sample II) of her husband, it will be seen how the SCARLET WOMAN card falls in the Head of the male counterpart and in the woman it is in the Heart. Since this card is in particular related to fecundity and the creative aspect of feminity it is quite clear where the psychological position rests in this couple. Generally it will be found that when *The Tantric Dakini Oracle* is used for a couple the two readings will complement each other.

$\mathcal{S}$ample IV

Mary, a bright young woman in her early twenties. Since she left college her life has taken a rather disjointed course. She has been torn between her allegiance to her father's wishes and her own desire for independence. This has been further complicated by her mother's suicide some time ago. The mother left her a large sum of money but also a heritage of guilt from which Mary finds it hard to escape. Her life has as yet no clear direction. There is confusion in her personal relationships coupled with an over-emphasis on the importance of material and financial power. These problems have prevented her from realizing her inherent potential (she is both psychic and intelligent). At the time of the reading she was taking a secretarial course, feeling the strain of city life and of the discipline needed for her to complete the course, and had not resolved her emotional situation. She asked *The Tantric Dakini Oracle* whether she should stay in the city, continuing in the direction started or whether to move out of the worldly situation. Two readings were made for her, one on the Map of the Great Universe and the other on the Tree of Life chart. The first reading, an astrological situation, is now dealt with in detail, and the Tree of Life positions are given afterward, adding to the understanding of her situation. Her astrological sign is Aries.

When making a reading on the Map of the Great Universe, (see Figure 12), the shuffling procedure is exactly as with the Tree of Life method, but the first card is placed on the location of Aries (the

Direct Reading onto the Map of the Great Universe

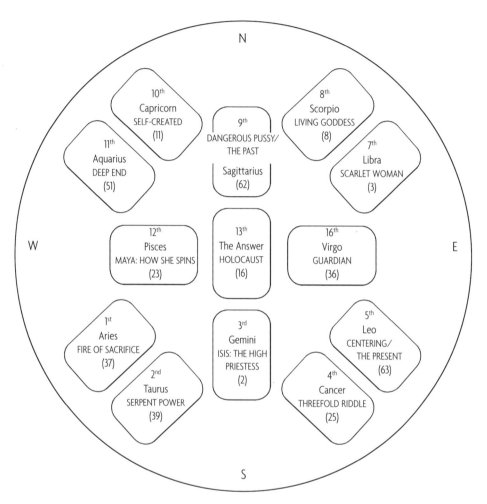

Figure 12. Mary's Cards on the Map of the Great Universe

first location, as marked) and then the next cards are turned over and placed in their locations consecutively. The thirteenth or last card is turned over and placed at the center of the diagram and represents *The Tantric Dakini Oracle*'s answer to the question. If no specific question has been asked then this central card represents the self of the questioner.

First card, position of Aries, the first house of the normal astrological chart. This is the place of personality, appearance, worldly outlook and potential. Here card 37, FIRE OF SACRIFICE, indicates the need to let go of all worldly clingings and habits through decisive action on the self. This is particularly relevant to Mary, whose Sun sign is Aries, suggesting that she needs to sacrifice self-interest in order to evolve and to gain real faith.

Second card, position of Taurus, as in the normal astrological chart. This is the place of financial affairs, material possessions and worldly stability. Here card 39, SERPENT POWER, indicates that Mary derives a sense of power from financial security. However this energy should be used in her case for transformation and should be creatively channeled if she wishes to achieve long-term fulfillment. This is a Fire card.

Third card, position of Gemini, the place of the intellect and communication, movement, both mental and physical. Here card 2, ISIS: THE HIGH PRIESTESS, a Major Arcana card, indicates a deep interest in the occult and the search for spiritual enlightenment. In this position it particularly points to the attainment of wishes through utilizing the intuitive female wisdom-nature of the intellect. Mary should set herself the highest goals and should apply her mind to that end. She should only move toward those who offer knowledge of this path.

Fourth card, position of Cancer, the place of the home environment, domestic affairs, the parents and the state of things at the close of life. Here card 25, THREEFOLD RIDDLE, an Air card, is located. This, as the Riddle card of the deck, has a deep personal meaning. In Mary's case the main element which has prevented her progress has been her ambivalent attachment to her parents. If this deep-seated emotional problem could be resolved then the ominous presence of the Riddle could be prevented from recurring at the end of her life. Mary must ruthlessly search her heart for that which has remained concealed, for only she has the power to liberate herself from this troublesome puzzle.

Fifth card, position of Leo, the fifth house of the normal astrological chart. This is the place of the heart, love affairs, pleasures, speculations and leadership. Here card 63, CENTERING/THE PRESENT is located. It is a Time card according to the method of *The Tantric Dakini Oracle* and represents the potent power of the here and now. It suggests that only from a position of self-centeredness (as opposed to selfishness) can any action have real meaning, and it tells that the moment to embark on any self-work is now. Mary cannot afford to let things slide any longer but should concentrate on centering on past problems to do with the emotions and relationships in the world. Thus she can gain transcendence over them in the present and consciously shape a real future.

Sixth card, position of Virgo, the place of health, work and food (both spiritual and physical). Here card 36, GUARDIAN, a Fire card, suggests the burning up of all illusory concepts and the acknowledgment of a guiding and protecting principle at work. The form of Mahakala on this card tells of the ability both to create and swallow up the patterns of destiny (karma). If Mary allows herself to be guided in an egoless way then she will be able to take nourishment from all activities, both in her work and from the people around her.

Seventh card, position of Libra, the seventh house of the normal astrological chart, the place of marriage, partnership, dealing with the public, enemies and balance. Here card 3, SCARLET WOMAN, is located, a Major Arcana card according to the system of the traditional Tarot and related to the Empress archetype. This card suggests that Mary has a strongly passionate nature. It indicates that she will find creative fulfillment only if she brings together the spirit and the body, using the concept of the Scarlet Woman as a touchstone for any liason. It tells of an-all-or nothing attitude toward lasting relationships and indicates that the finding of a partner will complete her on many levels, both physically and spiritually.

Eighth card, house of Scorpio, the place of the Occult, legacies, sex, taxes, money and death. Here card 8, LIVING GODDESS is located, a Major Arcana card depicting the earthly manifestations of spiritual ideals and duty toward such higher aspirations. In this position it denotes self-development to meet a position which one has been put in, needing dedication and resignation. Mary's legacies have put her in a certain position in the world which she now finds herself obliged to maintain. As this house also rules death, the suggestion is that she should place her commitment more toward her higher aspirations. She should work toward such a direction rather than letting any morbidity take over. For with her inherited legacies also come the taxes (both in the world and in the psyche) and this could become a vicious circle unless she can overcome it by acting as a Living Goddess herself. If she can explore the less temporal aspects of her life she will better be able to fulfill her duty to herself.

Ninth card, house of Sagittarius, the place of higher education, philosophy, religion, law, ideals and dreams. Here card 62, DANGEROUS PUSSY/THE PAST, is located. This is another Time card and in this position it suggests that Mary look toward the ancient truths and the esoteric teachings (the Tantric transmission) for her higher education. This is a very potent card, invoking the Past and stressing the need for right-minded action. If Mary is going to follow this path she must take full responsibility for herself. It is obviously her ideal, if she can be equal to it.

Tenth card, house of Capricorn, the place of profession, acclaim, ambition and the mother. Here card 11, SELF-CREATED, is located, a Major Arcana card according to the traditional Tarot system and related to Strength. This placement suggests that, for Mary to achieve her inner ambitions, she must become totally self-reliant, breaking with any ties to her mother. She must realize that she is self-created anyway and that she comes to this world through her own free will, through the karmic chain of cause and effect, which transcends lifetimes.

Eleventh card, house of Aquarius, the place of hopes, wishes, friends, associates and intellectual ideals. Here card 51, DEEP END, is located, a Water card. This card suggests a desire to abandon the restrictions made by the ego and to enter any situation with total adaptability. It shows Mary's aspiration to let herself go and be enveloped by any new situation without trying to hang on to any prejudices or predetermined ideas. She should plunge into the unconscious to find her hopes and aspirations and should give up any inner dialogue that stops her from doing this.

Twelfth card, house of Pisces, the place of restriction, karma, secret enemies, self-undoing and unexpected troubles. Here card 23, MAYA: HOW SHE SPINS, is located, an Air card. This card tells of the transient nature of all things. In this place on the Map of the Great Universe it warns Mary not to believe in all the passing phenomena of the world, such as ambition, name, fame, money and so forth. If she does then she will find herself caught up by her own weaving, for Maya is the controller of destiny (karma) and Mary should withdraw from attachment to the world if she wishes to know this spinner of the webs of illusion. If she can do this then she will control her own fate; otherwise, she will suddenly find herself restricted and may feel threatened.

The above completes the outer circle of the astrological reading. At the central position on the map, in the place marked 13, the questioner and the outcome of the question is represented. This is the Mount Meru of the mystic Universe, a mountain of gems with rivers flowing out at the four directions (North, South, East and West) toward the continents and sub-continents which make out the card positions and the astrological houses.

At the central position is card 16, HOLOCAUST, a Major Arcana card according to the Tarot system. This is a fire card, indicating the need to change one's position and to take dramatic action in order to rid oneself of all confusion caused by ego-motivation and worldly attachments. In Mary's reading the message is strong and clear, showing that the possibilities for self-growth are all there but that they can only be reached through making a deep change in psychological position. Mary must be prepared to lose those things to which she clings, and in this way she will be able to gain on a far deeper level. The saying "he who hesitates is lost" is very relevant here. Mary must assume an uncompromising and ruthless attitude toward her own personality, using shock tactics where necessary rather than letting apathy or laziness prevail.

The numerology of the astrological type of reading is worked out in the same way as in the Tree of Life reading. The twelve cards around the circumference at the positions of the astrological houses are added together. Thus, for Mary's reading we have: $37 + 39 + 2 + 25 + 63 + 36 + 3 + 8 + 62 + 11 + 51 + 23 = 360$ the number for the Influence cards. This is then added to the card number of the central position in this case 16, giving a total of 376 for the whole reading. These three digits, $3 + 7 + 6$ are then added together, giving the number sixteen, which is the number of the HOLOCAUST card already placed at the center. Thus it can be seen that the numerology of this reacting further accentuates the strength of the central card, pointing out the need for Mary to make a sudden drastic change, to leave her habitual patterns and move toward a lifestyle free from worldly attachments. The fact that the combined numbers of the circumference add up to 360 is of great interest here. For this is the number of degrees in a circle, suggesting here that all possibilities are available to her but that she must do the necessary self-work in order to overcome the Holocaust at her center.

Direct Reading onto Tree of Life Chart

In order to further develop the reading for Mary, a second consultation was made on the Tree of Life chart. This follows, with the position clearly outlined but not analyzed in detail. It can be seen that the outcome to the same question was card 41, HIGH TENSION. This card is in effect a corroboration of the validity of the reading on the Map of the Great Universe, for the divinatory meaning here is that the questioner needs to take a firm position, as a warrior. In the head location it tells of the need to temper the lifestyle so that it will not produce high tension in the mind. This concept is particularly related to the HOLOCAUST card, which says the same thing, but from the reference point of astrology (See Figure 13).

Mary was able to clearly understand her situation from the combination of these two readings. Each adds to the other and gives the direction along which the best results will be produced. The numerology of the two readings complement each other for the first one tells of the need to make a sudden drastic change, to leave habits, and the second tells of her need to take control of her own destiny, to take a position of responsibility.

The numerology of this reading is found by adding together the individual number of the cards. Thus 48 + 33 + 62 + 22 + 13 + 3 + 64 + 14 + 43 + 41 = 343. This number is then broken down and added together, 3 + 4 + 3 = 10, the overall number of the reading as related to the Tree of Life and the subtle body of the questioner. This number in *The Tantric Dakini Oracle* is the card WHEEL OF GREAT TIME, the brief divinatory meaning of which is the burning up of karma (by taking a conscious position), the completion of the cycle of destiny. The indication is for the person to take action. This will lead to success. This reading tells Mary that she should take responsibility for her own destiny and that she should do this by acting consciously and selflessly. This will lead her to success and transcendence of High Tension (the "outcome" card) that she is presently experiencing.

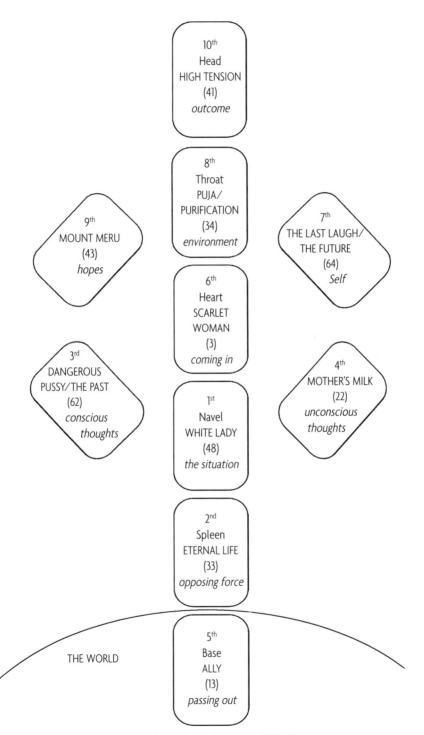

Figure 13. Mary's Cards on the Tree of Life Chart

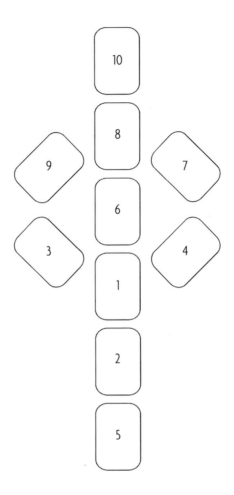

Card		Number	Card Title
1	the situation surrounding	_____	_____
2	opposing forces	_____	_____
3	conscious thoughts	_____	_____
4	unconscious thoughts	_____	_____
5	passing out influences	_____	_____
6	influences coming through	_____	_____
7	the self	_____	_____
8	the environment	_____	_____
9	hopes and expectations	_____	_____
10	final outcome, the answer	_____	_____

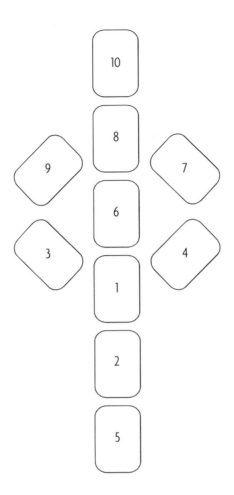

Card		Number	Card Title
1	the situation surrounding	_____	_____
2	opposing forces	_____	_____
3	conscious thoughts	_____	_____
4	unconscious thoughts	_____	_____
5	passing out influences	_____	_____
6	influences coming through	_____	_____
7	the self	_____	_____
8	the environment	_____	_____
9	hopes and expectations	_____	_____
10	final outcome, the answer	_____	_____

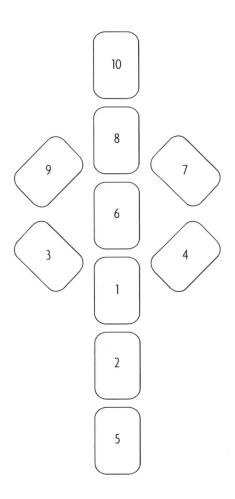

Card		Number	Card Title
1	the situation surrounding	_____	_____
2	opposing forces	_____	_____
3	conscious thoughts	_____	_____
4	unconscious thoughts	_____	_____
5	passing out influences	_____	_____
6	influences coming through	_____	_____
7	the self	_____	_____
8	the environment	_____	_____
9	hopes and expectations	_____	_____
10	final outcome, the answer	_____	_____

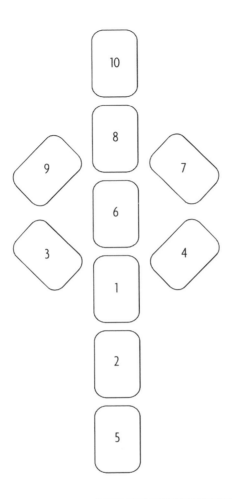

Card		Number	Card Title
1	the situation surrounding		
2	opposing forces		
3	conscious thoughts		
4	unconscious thoughts		
5	passing out influences		
6	influences coming through		
7	the self		
8	the environment		
9	hopes and expectations		
10	final outcome, the answer		

About the Authors

Nik Douglas was born in Yorkshire, England, but spent much of his childhood in the Middle East. From an early age he pursued knowledge of ancient cultures, specializing in Egyptology, ancient art, and occultism. He has traveled extensively in Asia, researching the spiritual beliefs and practices of Buddhism and Hinduism. He is a celebrated author, artist, and collector of Middle Eastern arts and antiquities. The majority of his career has been devoted to the study of tantra. He has studied with some of the foremost experts on Hindu and Tibetan tantra and helped organize the first major exhibit of tantra art at London's Hayward Gallery. He lives in Anguilla, British West Indies.

Penny Slinger is a multi-media artist and graduate of Chelsea College of Art, London. She has established herself as one of the world's leading visionary erotic artists and has gained international acclaim for her multi-faceted work. She has produced and directed several videos, including *Visions of the Arawaks* (1994), *Dance of the Cosmos* (2000), and her DVD *Goddess Juice* (2003). She spends her time manifesting the many forms of Goddess Tantra at the Goddess Temple in Northern California.

Tree of Life Chart and The Great Universe Map Ordering Information

The black-and-white photographs and schematic diagrams of the Tree of Life Chart and The Great Universe Map shown in this book are based on full-color collage paintings by artist Penny Slinger. The paintings are available in 26″ x 34″ color reproductions directly from the artist and can be used to take *The Tantric Dakini Oracle* experience to another level of self-reflection and divination.

The Tree of Life: The Subtle Body Chart (see cover image and description on pages 13–20). Use this chart for meditating upon the placement of your cards on the Tree of Life and to see how they line up with the energetic centers of your subtle body.

The Great Universe: An Astrological Map (see pages 20–23). With your cards in place on the map, meditate on this as a mandala of self, with all your tendencies described. Your essence is seated at the center, ready to shift to the next octave, but only when you have understood and integrated the influences present in your own psychic cosmogram. By your intention, you can direct the reading to reflect your basic characteristics as encoded at your birth through celestial influences, or look into a particular time cycle and see its unfoldment.

For more information on how to obtain these full color reproductions, go to www.PennySlinger.com/prints.

BOOKS OF RELATED INTEREST

Sexual Secrets: Twentieth Anniversary Edition
The Alchemy of Ecstasy
by Nik Douglas and Penny Slinger

**The Erotic Sentiment in the
Paintings of India and Nepal**
by Nik Douglas and Penny Slinger

Tools for Tantra
by Harish Johari

Tantric Orgasm for Women
by Diana Richardson

Tantric Quest
An Encounter with Absolute Love
by Daniel Odier

Womb Wisdom
Awakening the Creative and Forgotten
Powers of the Feminine
by Padma and Anaiya Aon Prakasha

**Sacred Geometry Cards
for the Visionary Path**
by Francene Hart

The Way of Tarot
The Spiritual Teacher in the Cards
by Alejandro Jodorowsky and Marianne Costa

Inner Traditions • Bear & Company
P.O. Box 388
Rochester, VT 05767
1-800-246-8648
www.InnerTraditions.com

Or contact your local bookseller